STUDY SKILLS FOR COLLEGE ATHLETES

BY
WALTER PAUK, PH.D.

H&H PUBLISHING COMPANY
CLEARWATER, FLORIDA

H&H Publishing Company, Inc.

1231 Kapp Drive
Clearwater, FL 33765
(727) 442-7760
(800) 366-4079
FAX (727) 442-2195
e-mail HHService@HHPublishing.com
www.HHPublishing.com

STUDY SKILLS FOR COLLEGE ATHLETES

Walter Pauk, Ph.D.

Production Supervisor
Robert D. Hackworth

Editing/Production
Karen Hackworth

Editorial Assistant
Priscilla Trimmier

Business Operations
Mile Ealy, Sally Marston

Acknowledgments

Excerpts from THE AUTOBIOGRAPHY OF MALCOLM X by Malcolm X, with the assistance of Alex Haley.
Copyright (c) 1964 by Alex Haley and Malcolm X.
Copyright (c) 1965 by Alex Haley and Betty Shabazz.
Reprinted by permission of Random House, Inc.

Excerpts reprinted courtesy of *SPORTS ILLUSTRATED*.
Copyright©, Time Inc.
All rights reserved.

ISBN 0-943202-69-8

Library of Congress Catalog Number 96-072549

Revised from a previous edition published by Reston-Stuart Publishing Company, 1986.

Printing is the lowest number: 10 9 8 7 6 5 4 3 2

PREFACE

TO STUDENTS

Coaches are 100% correct! They know by instinct and by experience that success in the classroom depends mainly on two interrelated characteristics: *control of time* and *self-discipline*.

Time. Everyone (rich or poor, king or peasant, miser or wastrel, deserving or undeserving, athlete or non-athlete)—everyone receives 24 golden hours every day. No one receives one minute more, nor one minute less. That's equality!

Equality in hours, yes! Yet, around us, we see students who achieve twice as much as others. How come? What's the secret?

This part of the secret is obvious. The achievers are self-disciplined. They're in complete control. In the library, for example, there's no wasting of time such as sitting and watching others. No! They head for the computer, find the books they need and go right to work extracting information for a term paper, for instance. Whatever the task, some productive work begins immediately.

"What a dull life!" you might say. No, not at all. In the late afternoon, you'll find them on the tennis court; or, in the evening, at a movie or the theater—*and* without any feeling of guilt, because they've done their work, and now they have time to play.

The other part of the secret is not so obvious but it's this: self-discipline and time management are essential for success but they are still not enough. The magic is when self-discipline and time management are coupled with *strategies* and *skills*, just as in sports. Then, you've got it made.

What strategies? Included in this book are two administraions of the **Learning and Study Strategies Inventory** (**LASSI**), an assessment for accurately determining your study strengths and weaknesses. You will take the first **LASSI** to give you a picture of your needs when entering this course. The second **LASSI** will tell you how much improvement has been made.

What skills? Well, in these thirteen chapters, you'll find the skills you need for academic success. You'll learn how to take notes in class, how to read a textbook, how to study for and take exams, how to write a paper, plan your time, improve your concentration, strengthen your memory, build your vocabulary, and many more tips and techniques on how to be a successful student.

This book is intended to help you be a success in college, not only athletically, but academically as well. Student athletes deal with a myriad of problems that non-athletes do not encounter. You have an athletic schedule as well as an academic schedule. You have a focus that involves your sport, as well as your education. You need skills to help you be successful in both areas of your college life.

To Instructors

Three additions have been added to this new version of *Study Skills for College Athletes*: two **LASSIs** (**Learning and Study Strategies Inventory**) for pre-and post-assessment, Word Interest, and Setting Goals.

Word Interest

New to this edition is a section in Chapter 1 on the Word History System, intended to create for students a personal interest in words. Of special interest is a case study about Malcolm X, using excerpts from his autobiography. This material reveals his vivid interest in education, and in particular, words.

Vocabulary pages end each chapter, using excerpts from *Sports Illustrated*.

Students have to have an interest in words to improve vocabulary. Interest is the keystone to the entire process. Even though we, as instructors, firmly believe in the interest principle, our problem remains: how to transmit the interest principle into the minds and hearts of our students.

The Word History System has worked in the academic lives of many students. It worked to create a personal interest in words. But, often, this interest remained within the confines of the academic world.

Here's what worked. Students were shown how this nascent interest could build their vocabularies many fold once it burst out of the academic world and rubbed shoulders with the mundane world of newspapers and magazines.

To demonstrate, a newspaper was brought in. The sporting page was exposed to an article reporting on the 1997 World Series. The first paragraph read—

> Rookie Jaret Wright threw a big-time heat on a wet, cold field Wednesday night to give Cleveland a 10-3 win against Florida that evened the World Series after four games.[1]

But the pin-pointed lesson here was the large-lettered headline that read—

ALL GOES WRIGHT FOR INDIANS

Yogi Berra was correct when he said, "You can observe a lot if you look."

When students see a headline like this, henceforth they will say to themselves, "How clever and how appropriate." Once students see and say this, they cannot help in the future from admiring and appreciating a writer's skillfulness and creativeness with words. This interest in words will not be confined only to the sports page. Interest will flow to any page that has mind-catching words. Here's an example dealing with finance. The paragraph reads—

> Robert Morrison was named CEO of Quaker Oats Thursday, one day after resigning as CEO of Kraft Foods.[2]

The headline introducing this article—

FEELING HIS OATS

Again, creative and appropriate.

Obvious Suggestion
Encourage students to bring in examples of headlines cleverly crafted.

After cutting their teeth on short clever headlines, students easily move on to longer writings, which also begin with innovative headings. Below is an article brought in by a student:

> Alamogordo, N.M. – Amid spiky yuccas and cholla cactus, a dry desert wind snaps the American flag above the tombstone of this U.S. Air Force veteran. "Ham," the inscription says, "world's first astrochimp."
>
> It's an odd resting place for a chimpanzee born in the dense rain forest of the Cameroons. But there's little about this chimp's life that wasn't strange. Trained aboard a Mercury capsule, rocketed into space, featured on the cover of *LIFE* magazine, Ham—short for Holloman Aero-Medical Laboratory—made history before the age of four.[3]

{ Perfect setting. "snaps" gives reader a sound.

{ "Astrochimp? What's that?"

{ Catches interest; read full story.

The headline—

MILITARY FINDS IT HAS MONKEY ON ITS BACK

Once students start to marvel at the skillfulness of a writer, they will no longer just read for information. Yes, they'll still read for information, but they'll also see how words can be used to convey that information interestingly and perhaps beautifully. By paying attention to how the information is being presented with words, students will be doing themselves a great favor: increasing their vocabularies almost effortlessly and enjoyably. This personal interest-technique of vocabulary development borders on the edge of wisdom; that is, "seeing things from the inside out."

Helping Students to Set Goals

Also in this edition is an expanded section on setting goals (Chapter 1).

Simply telling a student to have a goal is not enough. You cannot force a goal on a person. Yes, they hear you, understand you, and agree with you. That does not mean they will internalize it—drink it in. We all know the adage, "You can lead a horse to water, but you can't make him drink."

Unwritten goals are in the same never-never land as dreams. Unwritten goals are bound to be fuzzy and unlikely to materialize. The magic of writing out a goal is that one creates a definite, sharp image of the goal, which is then not only focused in the conscious mind, but also incubates in the subconscious mind, taking shape and becoming real. John Wooten, famous UCLA basketball coach, sums it up by saying, "Failing to plan is planning to fail."

One thing that almost all successful people have in common is that their goals are written out in detail. In the following example, this person had something even better than a written-out goal. He had a picture.

> Conrad Hilton, who was on the verge of bankruptcy in 1931, cut out a picture of the Waldorf Hotel in New York City, and put it under the cracked and chipped glasstop of his desk. He gazed at this picture every day. Eighteen years later, Conrad Hilton acquired the Waldorf.

Goal setting is a hard thing to do. Why? I think because it has a deep emotional dimension. To help students set goals, we must somehow touch not only their minds, but also their hearts.

There's no easy way. There is no SQ3R for setting goals—no cut and dried formula. With goal setting, we, as teachers, are truly touching the vital lives of our students. I think one approach to helping our students is to inspire them to plumb their own depths and to do the goal setting in a personal, serious way. I believe that for a goal to be a driving force, it must have this honest, personal quality. As I see it, the words from Frank Sinatra's song, "My Way," are not a selfish, unthinking expression of a person egotistically forcing his or her will upon another. Rather, they are an expression—"I have one life to live, it's precious, and I want to live it the way that will best fulfill what I am meant to be."

Not too long ago, in one of the inner sections of the *Wall Street Journal*, there was a feature article titled something like this: "Changing Careers in Mid-Life." What impressed me about this article is the high percentage of people who changed careers—around 43%.

How does the article relate to goals? One thought is that they did not make the right choice in the first place. Of course, they are many reasons for changing careers. However, I think that the reading of such articles by a class of students, followed by a class discussion the next day, would impress upon students the long-term seriousness of doing the job of goal setting. In discussion, the ideas could come from the students themselves, all with varying opinions, rather than being imposed upon from the instructor.

I am convinced that a discussion method, based on good, sound readings, is the first necessary step to take in getting across the importance of goal-setting to a class of students. After this discussion, present graphic steps that a student can take to evolve his/ her own goals.

It is a good idea to include an article about being realistic about choosing one's goals. It is as foolish to set one's mark too high as it is to set it too low. Students must decide for themselves. And, however one sets a goal, adjustments can be made along the way.

In all class discussions, the dominate refrain should be, "Take realistic action!"

Barbara Hoese, at her high school valedictory address, said, ". . . some people make things happen; some people watch things happen; and some people don't know anything happened."[4]

This theme of action coincides with this ancient Chinese anecdote of wisdom:

"He who stand with mouth open, wait long time before roast duck fly in."

So, students must see that they must make things happen.

NOTES

[1] Rod Beaton, Sports, *USA TODAY* 23 October 1997: C1.

[2] *USA TODAY*, Money 24 October 1997: B1.

[3] *The Wall Street Journal* 30 December 1997: A1.

[4] Richard J. Leider, *The Power of Purpose* (San Francisco: Berrett-Koehler Publishers, Inc., 1997) 98-99.

CONTENTS

Placing an equal emphasis on academics and athletics, and implementing study skills and time management programs, has raised our overall teams' GPA significantly. I am convinced that athletic performance and academic performance go hand-in-hand.

JAY VIDOVICH, *Head Men's Soccer Coach, Wake Forest University*

1
BECOMING A SUCCESS

After a storm, an Indian boy found an eagle's egg. Instantly, he knew what to do with it. Cupping the egg in his hands, he ran swiftly to put it into a prairie chicken's warm nest.

The eaglet grew up with the rest of the chicks. Thinking it was a prairie chicken, it did what they did; scratched the dirt for seeds and insects, and fluttered awkwardly about.

One day, when the eaglet was half-grown, it saw a magnificent bird high in the sky, soaring effortlessly with hardly a movement of its golden wings.

"What a magnificent bird," said the eaglet to an elder prairie chicken. "What is it?" "That's an eagle, king of the birds. But don't get any big ideas. Prairie chickens can never fly like that."

The poor eaglet never did give the idea a second thought. It continued to scratch in the dirt, walk around rocks, and awkwardly flutter over thick sage brush.

Finally, it grew old and died, thinking to the last that it was a prairie chicken.

There's some eagle in all of us. Maybe we can't all soar; but, at least we don't have to keep scratching the dirt for seeds and fluttering through life like prairie chickens—so don't walk when you can fly.

THE PRAIRIE CHICKEN

This story is to remind us that we should sit down and assess our strengths, and on such a basis make plans for our futures. We must construct our future in terms of goals. When written out, goals give us direction, strength, determination, and commitment. Without goals, we can go on through life scratching in the dirt and never flying, although we could have, perhaps, flown if we had planned and tried.

Look what *"Pikes Peak or Bust"* did for the early pioneers who painted this goal on the sides of their covered wagons. These words showed the inner determination of every man and woman to keep going, never to give up.

Humans somehow gain strength from goals. It seems that goals are most needed when the going gets tough. Goals keep a person from quitting. But, when things get tough, it is too late to sit down calmly and form a goal. A goal must be thought out and written *before* you begin the academic semester and before you go out for your first practice.

WRITE OUT YOUR GOALS

Repeatedly you've been encouraged to "sit down and write out what your goals in life are." So, you sit at your desk, haul out a blank sheet of paper, and often, even after an hour, the sheet is still blank.

Everyone knows it is not easy, even people in business. Warren Malkerson, Vice President of a large catalogue house said, "Every human is struggling to unlock his or her potential."[1]

The log-jam of thoughts needs to be broken. How? By almost immediately writing the first goal-thought that enters your mind. Then, continue writing, one after another without analyzing any of them. After listing all that entered your mind, begin to analyze each one. Draw a line through those that do not stand up to analysis. Transfer the survivors to a clean sheet of paper, then continue your analysis of each again, crossing out any not meeting your criteria. Somehow, you must boil the list down to a final Gibraltar-like goal. The secret of this process is to make a list first, then make judgmental analyses.

"Don't feel that you have to follow the crowd. You are unique. You're one of a kind. Therefore, you must fashion your own goal to fit your unique talents. Often the trickiest part of getting what you want out of life is figuring out what it *is* you want. When you ask people, 'What do you want out of life?' it often boils down to two things: work and love."[2]

Some goals are long-term and some are short-term. For example, I like Junior Seau's short-term goal, which could also be a long-term goal. He can use it game by game, season by season, and for the rest of his football career.

> *"I'm playing every down like it's the most important I'll ever play.*
> *If I can't be that player, no matter what the record is, believe me,*
> *I'll hang up the helmet."*[3]

A Few Examples

No need for a fancy essay. Just a few sentences stating your goals, both long-term and short-term. Write your goals now.

1. What's your long-term goal in athletics?
    Example*: To become a first-string player in my second year.*

    _____

    _____

    _____

2. What's your short-term goal in athletics?
    Example*: To learn everything about my position and to increase my strength through exercise.*

    _____

    _____

    _____

3. What's your long-term academic goal?
   Example: *To get a degree in business (in science, in agriculture, in engineering, etc.).*

   _____

   _____

4. What's your short-term academic goal?
   Example: *To get better-than-average grades this first semester.*

   _____

   _____

VISUALIZE YOUR GOALS

Plan your goals in your mind so that you can mentally see them. The power of visualization is largely unknown to most people; but, the ones who know about it use it all the time for various goals and purposes.

Look how Jason Elam, the Denver Bronco's place-kicker uses it.

Elam can see winning kick

SAN DIEGO – Denver place-kicker Jason Elam already is playing the final minutes of Super Bowl XXXII in his mind.

"I've already been over every possible situation in my head, what could possibly happen," Elam says.

The five-year veteran envisions kicks from different angles and distances under varying conditions at Qualcomm Stadium. "Visualization is huge for a kicker," he says.

In his mind's eye, the image is always the same. He trots onto the field and checks the flag poles to gauge the wind. He reminds himself for a final time to stay calm, maintain a strong plant foot and swing straight through the ball. Then he steps off the kick, follows the checklist and drives the ball through the middle of the uprights.

That's the plan, anyway. Elam views Super Bowl XXXII as a chance to atone for a disappointing regular season in which he hit 26 of 36 field goal attempts and was 3-for-8 between the 40- and 49-yard lines.

"Jason wants to be perfect," Broncos coach Mike Shanahan says, "and the big thing is to be perfect the next game."

By Tom Pedulla

USA TODAY. Wednesday, January 21, 1998, page 4C.

A Final Word

A well-planned, visualized goal can carry you through some trying times, which are bound to come to everyone. Jim Dines says, "Only those who have built their ark in advance will weather the storm."[4]

Professional Athletics

If your goal is to become a professional athlete, that's fine. But, this shouldn't mean that you should forget about academics. Perhaps you can gain some wisdom from knowing how some other athletes handled the decision-making problem. Let's start with Baron Davis.

> These days, the question hovers over all impact freshmen, including UCLA's Baron Davis, the most coveted of this year's point guard recruits. Like most of his classmates, Davis becomes uncharacteristically hesitant when discussing his basketball future. He has seen riches and glory accrue to those who jumped at the right time, but he knows disappointment can be the lot of those who leave school too early. "I have no time-table," say Davis. "At the moment my goal is to graduate. I would like to stay four years. But it depends on if I feel mature enough and feel physically and mentally ready to play against the best competition in the world."[5]

Looking Farther Down the Road

Here's a person who has earned a Super Bowl ring with the San Francisco Forty-Niners. Yet, he knows that football is not forever. Derrick Harmon says,

> *"I love playing football but, as always, I'm looking farther down the road. That's why I'm here at Cornell taking graduate courses during football's off-season. You have to be realistic and plan for the future."*[6]

Carnell Lake, all-pro strong safety for the Pittsburgh Steelers, amazes me and gains my utmost respect. Here is a man earning good money. Yet, during the off-season, like Derrick Harmon, he puts his trust in academics by taking night classes in accounting at Duquesnes University. Notice that he's taking a down-to-earth subject, perhaps to gain a business foundation for some future venture.

Then there's Gino Torretta, the former University of Miami quarterback and 1992 Heisman Trophy winner, who finished his academic work for a degree before entering the pros. He had good opportunities, but was waived eight times by five teams. Yet, he hasn't given up hope. Evidently, he's highly respected as a quality player. Here's an excerpt from *SPORTS ILLUSTRATED*.

> The Colts signed Torretta as an emergency quarterback on Nov. 11, 1997. He suited up for the following Sunday's upset of the Packers and collected $11,529, but the Colts released him the following day, and he returned to his job at a Boca Raton investment company.[7]

Notice, Gino Torretta, because of his academic degree, has a good job to fall back on while still waiting for another opportunity in pro-football.

"To be, or not to be," characterizes Hamlet's state of mind while pondering a decision. Some students are in Hamlet's shoes: finishing school or throwing oneself into the draft of professional sports.

Maybe Benjamin Franklin's wise words can be of some help during the decision-making process:

If a man empties his purse into his head, no one can take it away from him. An investment in knowledge always pays the best interest.

Evidently Derrick Harmon, Carnell Lake, and Gino Torretta see it Franklin's way.

This book was written to help you develop effective and efficient study skills so that you can become a success in whatever you do.

THE WORD HISTORY SYSTEM

In this edition, a new vocabulary development program, the Word History System, is being introduced for the first time. This System came about one summer session while teaching a class of thirty college-bound senior high school students. Just by chance, I found a method for launching almost everyone on a sharply upward curve.

Having just one copy of *Interesting Origins of English Words*, I would loan the book to each of the thirty students, one at a time, for just one over-night period. The next morning the book was handed to another student. The results—scores on the final standardized vocabulary test, when compared to the pre-test, were all in the very top percentiles. I was convinced I had discovered, by chance, a system that could help all students who would give this Word History System a fair try.

To use the Word History System, turn to Chapter 6, Building Your Vocabulary, where the word *agony* is illustrated by two men wrestling. Such a picture impresses the mind with the word's history. The explanation of the word *agony* answers the question, "I wonder where that word came from?" If you ask such a question, you are almost guaranteed to develop a fine, large vocabulary, because you'll now have on your side the powerful mental attitude of *interest in words*.

Word interest is forever and the Word History System is one of the best ways to help you create and internalize an interest, perhaps a love, for words. Once you become genuinely interested in words, you will pay attention to words both printed and spoken. Even in ordinary words you will marvel at the ingenuity of people who name a company U-HAUL, which says everything.

One day, while shopping for a moisturizing cream, I was bewildered by the vast array of brands. I picked up a plastic jar with white and black, irregular spots, looking like the hide of a Jersey cow. I know about "cow cream." People who milk cows rarely have chapped hands. Why? After milking a cow, the farmer applies a cream to the cow's udder to keep the skin soft and supple. With the remaining cream on his or her hands, they simply rub it into their own skin. Well, the jar I had picked up (and eventually bought out of delight) was named "Udderly Smooth." And to add another facet, the word "smooth" had three letters larger and darker, MOO!

When you delight in such small things, you're lucky. You'll be genuinely interested in words, and this genuine interest will propel you to intellectual heights.

At this chapter's end, and after each subsequent chapter, you will find one page devoted entirely to vocabulary development. The top of the page is very important. You have the history of one word. Once you have the history—the background for that word—you will be able to remember the word and use it not only properly, but also with more precision. Unfortunately, we don't have a picture to go with each word. I suggest you read the word histories and then try to picture in your mind how you would illustrate the word in a book if you were the artist.

After all, the artist who etched the picture of agony had to go through a similar process. You may not have the talent to draw the picture, but your mind has the talent to visualize what a picture could be like as constructed by your imagination. The picture that you create in your imagination will have a long-lasting quality. You'll be implanting the word's history in your long-term memory.

On the rest of the vocabulary page, you will find several separate, interesting passages, all taken from recent issues of *SPORTS ILLUSTRATED*. In each passage, you'll find one word or several words italicized. You are asked to select, from two options, the meaning for each word as it is used in context.

This is in no way a test. Rather, the purpose is to expose you to words currently used in writing. Some of the words you'll already know but will be good reinforcement. For the unfamiliar words, you'll get the chance to put them on vocabulary cards for further study.

A POWERFUL CASE HISTORY: MALCOLM X

I heard somewhere some time ago that Malcolm X developed a powerful vocabulary while serving time in a penitentiary. I immediately became interested in how he did it so I could pass on to you his techniques and system.

But first, let me refresh your memories by providing you with a short sketch of this remarkable man.

His given name was Malcolm Little. He was born in 1925 and died in 1965, living a short forty years. He was an American Black activist and a member of the Black Muslims (1952-1963). He advocated separatism and Black pride. After converting to orthodox Islam, he founded the Organization of Afro-American Unity (1964) and was assassinated, by another Black, in Harlem.

Through the following series of excerpts from his *Autobiography*, written with the help of Alex Haley, let me show you how Malcolm X developed from a near-illiterate to a highly intelligent, powerful speaker.

Acknowledgment
From THE AUTOBIOGRAPHY OF MALCOLM X by
Malcolm X, with the assistance of Alex Haley.
Copyright (c) 1964 by Alex Haley and Malcolm X.
Copyright (c) 1965 by Alex Haley and Betty Shabazz.
Reprinted by permission of Random House, Inc.

We first find Malcolm X in Harlem as a hustler. A hustler was a person who really knew the "ropes." He could do just about any illegal job that anyone desired. In his own words, he describes his status as follows:

There I was back in Harlem's streets among all the rest of the hustlers. I couldn't sell reefers; the dope squad detectives were too familiar with me. I was a true hustler—uneducated, unskilled at anything honorable, and I considered myself nervy and cunning enough to live by my wits, exploiting any prey that presented itself. I would risk just about anything.

From hustling he worked up to robberies. Here's his story:

During the next six to eight months, I pulled my first robberies and stick-ups. Only small ones. Always in other, nearby cities. And I got away.

Inevitably, he was caught and sent to the penitentiary. While there, he would get letters from his brother and sister; but, he was unable to answer the letters because he couldn't write a sentence, nor could he spell. He felt helpless. Here's his confession about his knowledge of words:

When I had finished the eighth grade back in Mason, Michigan, that was the last time I'd thought of studying anything that didn't have some hustle purpose. And the streets had erased everything I'd ever learned in school: I didn't know a verb from a house.

Now came the turning point in Malcolm X's life. This was the great critical incident, which came by miraculous chance. In the penitentiary, the prisoners had jobs, such as stamping out license plates. During his spare time, he was exceedingly fortunate to listen to Bimbi, a black man who had been in the penitentiary a long time and who spent all his spare hours in the library reading and studying. Here's the critical incident:

When he (Bimbi) talked about the history of Concord, where I was to be transferred later, you would have thought he was hired by the Chamber of Commerce, and I wasn't the first inmate who had never heard of Thoreau until Bimbi expounded upon him. Bimbi was known as the library's best customer. What fascinated me with him most of all was that he was the first man I had ever seen command total respect . . . with his words.

Other men commanded respect because of their strength, their cunningness, the number of robberies committed, and so forth. But, Bimbi commanded respect with his speech, with his words. Malcolm X had not only heard Bimbi's words, he had *internalized* a strong desire to be like Bimbi—to learn words and language:

> *It had really begun back in the Charlestown Prison, when Bimbi first made me feel envy of his stock of knowledge. Bimbi had always taken charge of any conversation he was in, and I had tried to emulate him. But every book I picked up had new sentences which didn't contain anywhere from one to nearly all of the words that might as well have been in Chinese. When I just skipped those words, of course, I really ended up with little idea of what the book said . . . pretty soon, I would have to quit . . . unless I had received the motivation that I did.*
>
> *I saw that the best thing I could do was get hold of a dictionary . . .*
>
> *I spent two days just riffling uncertainly through the dictionary's pages. I'd never realized so many words existed! I just didn't know **which** words to learn. Finally, just to start some kind of action, I began copying.*
>
> *In my slow, painstaking, ragged handwriting, I copied into my tablet everything printed on that first page, down to the punctuation marks.*
>
> *I believe it took me a day. Then, aloud, I read back, to myself, everything I'd written on the tablet. Over and over, aloud, to myself, I read my own handwriting.*
>
> *I woke up the next morning thinking about those words . . .*

Malcolm X became so fascinated with words that he eventually copied the entire dictionary. Finally, Malcolm X had this to say for his dictionary-reading efforts:

> *I suppose it was inevitable that as my word-base broadened, I could for the first time pick up a book and read and now begin to understand what the book was saying. Anyone who has read a great deal can imagine the new world that opened.*

Starting almost from scratch—learning from the dictionary—Malcolm X, through constant reading, finally reached a high point in the knowledge of words—a point to which any person would be proud. He reached philology—the study of words. Here's Malcolm X again, talking to Alex Haley:

> *"People don't realize how a man's whole life can be changed by one book."*
> *He came back again and again to the book that he had studied when in prison.*
> *"Did you ever read The Loom of Language?" he asked me, and I said I hadn't.*
> *"You should. Philology, it's a tough science—all about how words can be recog-*

nized, no matter where you find them. Now, you take 'Caesar,' it's Latin. In Latin it's pronounced like 'Kaiser,' with a hard C. But we Anglicize it by pronouncing a soft C. The Russians say 'Czar' and mean the same thing. Another Russian dialect says 'Tsar.' Jakob Grimm was one of the foremost philologists, I studied his 'Grimm's Law' in prison—all about consonants. Philology is related to the science of etymology, dealing in root words. I dabbled in both of them."

Malcolm X did more than 'dabble' in the study of words. He either shaped his life around words, or the words took over and shaped his life. Either way, he was a winner—he became a "thinking man." This almost obsession with words is illustrated beautifully by this excerpt, which came from Alex Haley's two-year interview with Malcolm X. This incident occurred when Malcolm X was proofreading the manuscript of his *Autobiography*.

Again when reading about the period when he had discovered the prison library, Malcolm X's head jerked up. "Boy! I never will forget that old aardvark!" The next evening, he came into the room and told me that he had been to the Museum of Natural History and learned something about the aardvark. "Now, aardvark actually means 'earth hog.' That's a good example of root words, as I was telling you. When you study the science of philology, you learn the laws governing how a consonant can lose its shape, but it keeps its identity from language to language." What astonished me here was that I know that on that day, Malcolm X's schedule had been crushing, involving both a television and radio appearance and a live speech, yet he had gone to find out something about the aardvark.

Malcolm X went on to become an outstanding preacher and public speaker. With a wide and exact vocabulary, he was able to express his thoughts and ideas forcefully and intelligently. He earned and commanded respect.

A FINAL WORD

Malcolm X has opened the door to intellectual growth to all of us. I hope this book helps you, through hard, concentrated study, open many doors—not only in athletics, but in life—through academic study and success.

VOCABULARY: BUILDING A BACKGROUND

Definition: ab-ra-ca-dab-ra—1. A magical charm or incantation having the power to ward off disease or disaster. 2. Foolish or unintelligible talk.

WORD HISTORY: *Abracadabra* was a magic word, the letters of which were arranged in an inverted pyramid and worn as an amulet around the neck to protect the wearer against disease or trouble. One fewer letter appeared in each line of the triangle, until only "a" remained to form the vertex of the triangle. As the letters disappeared, so supposedly did the disease or trouble. While magicians still use *abracadabra* in their performances, the word itself has acquired another sense, "foolish and unintelligible talk."

ABRACADABRA
ABRACADABR
ABRACADAB
ABRACADA
ABRACAD
ABRACA
ABRAC
ABRA
ABR
AB
A

WORDS IN CONTEXT

Directions: Make a light check mark (✓) alongside one of the two words (choices) that most nearly expresses the meaning of the italicized word in the episodes. (Answers are given on p. 126.) Excerpts reprinted courtesy of *SPORTS ILLUSTRATED*. Copyright ©, Time Inc. All rights reserved.

As the Dallas Cowboys' offense sputters, questions run *rampant*. The foremost: Are Emmitt Smith's best days behind him? Here's Emmitt's answer: "I can feel a difference in my game. Maybe I don't have the burst I had four years ago. But who's the same player he was four years ago? I know this: There's a lot more great football left in me. No way do I think I'm at the end."

1.	questions run *rampant*	wild	quickly

Washington Redskins: Michael Westbrook's friends rise in his defense. They *concede* that he was *impulsive* and wrong to yank off his helmet in the heat of battle, but that he was responding from the heart. Their biggest fear is that Westbrook will never escape the shadow of his recent *transgression*.

2.	they *concede*	deny	admit
3.	he was *impulsive*	rash	cautious
4.	his recent *transgression*	merit	offense

Coach Jerry Rhome, offensive coordinator for the St. Louis Rams, *abides* by this coaching *principle*: "Coaching not only *involves* showing players how to do something. It's explaining why we do it."

5.	*abides* by	stands	judges
6.	this coaching *principle*	rule	habit
7.	not only *involves*	conspires	entails

NOTES

[1] Richard J. Leider, *The Power of Purpose* (San Francisco, Berrett-Koehler Publishers, Inc., 1997) 101-102.

[2] Richard J. Leider, *The Power of Purpose* (San Francisco, Berrett-Koehler Publishers, Inc., 1997) 63.

[3] *Sports Illustrated*, 22 December 1997: 127.

[4] James Dines, *The Dines Letter*, PO Box 22, Belevedere, CA 94920, December 5, 1997.

[5] *Sports Illustrated*, 15 December 1997: 85.

[6] Personal interview.

[7] *Sports Illustrated*, 15 December 1997: 90.

"Unfortunately, academics seems to be less of a priority when it comes to student-athletes in today's college environment. More and more emphasis is put on winning on the field rather than winning in the classroom. In the long run, intellectual growth and maturity is far more valuable than a win-loss record. What good are accolades when you don't even know what that word means."

APRIL KATER, *Head Women's Soccer Coach, Syracuse University*

Build a Strong Foundation

I spent more time studying during my freshman year than any year after that. In this way, I built up a large reserve of pacts and principles that I used during the other three years. For example, I always studied more deeply for an exam than was necessary. I avoided any narrow emphasis. I was always looking farther down the road.

Scheduling Time—Everybody's Different

Never mind what other people do. Identify your own pluses and minuses. Work on the minuses! I knew I functioned best early in the morning; so, I always studied an hour or two before classes started. Engineering is demanding, so I had to make every hour count. There could be no wasted hours.

Always Have a Goal

Goals, however, often change. This is okay, but, immediately set another goal to shoot for.

The Future is Through Education

I love playing football; but, as always, I'm looking farther down the road. That's why I'm here at Cornell taking graduate courses during football's off-season. You have to be realistic and plan for the future.

DERRICK HARMON, *Cornell University Engr. '83; former San Francisco Forty-Niner*

2
YOUR HEALTH

"Some mornings, I'm just too tired to think, even if I've gotten plenty of sleep." Is this you?

DRAGGED OUT. When you feel dragged out and even find it hard to think, it's probably not a matter of being low on sleep; rather, the chances are great that your blood sugar is low.

BLOOD SUGAR? Yes. You see, blood sugar (also known as glucose) is what your body's cells use to produce energy. You get this blood sugar from the food you eat.

Portions of all foods are turned into blood sugar. But, here's the catch: foods such as candy, donuts, and sweets in general produce too much sugar too quickly. When too much sugar suddenly enters your bloodstream, an alarm triggers your pancreas to send out a flood of insulin to cut the sugar level down. More often than not, the pancreas overreacts, sending out too much insulin. As a result, your blood sugar drops to a level below what you started with and you're left feeling weaker than you did before you began eating.

PREVENTION. The way to keep your system from overreacting is to add some protein, especially to your breakfast. Proteins are converted into glucose at a slower pace so your body gets a slower and steadier amount of blood sugar. Because the sugar is added gradually, the insulin alarm isn't triggered, and you get the energy you need for a longer period of time.

COFFEE AND
DONUTS.
A breakfast of coffee and donuts is almost as bad as no breakfast at all. Sure, they'll cause a rapid rise in blood sugar, which will give you a *brief* feeling of energy; but, in no time at all your blood sugar will plunge below the original level, leaving you weak and wrung out for much of the day.

CANDY BARS.
As we know, candy bars are full of sugar; so, don't eat one as a substitute for good food, either during class hours, study hours, or before or during an athletic game. To make the point about sugar and insulin, this story is often told.

> Before a basketball game, for instance, appear to be generous by giving each player on the opposing team a couple of candy bars. Of course, if they eat the bars, they'll feel light and full of energy because their blood stream is full of sugar, which triggers the pancreas to pour in insulin to counteract the excess sugar. And, as usual, the insulin metabolizes not only the new sugar, but also the sugar that was already there; thus, leaving the players with less energy-producing blood-sugar than what they had before eating the candy. The players on the opposing team are now dragged out—not so light and not so energetic. Obviously, it's easier to beat a dragged out team than a team with regular blood sugar to provide energy to play vigorously. Of course, it would be unsportsmanlike to pull off such a trick.

Eating the right foods and staying away from the wrong foods are all important to good health. Some people seem to live just for today, not thinking about tomorrow. For example, a front-page article in the *Wall Street Journal* describes the start of a marathon race in New Orleans, just before Mardi Gras:

> . . . a runner takes a long last drag on his cigarette. Another one carbo-loads this city's famous breakfast food: fried blobs of sugary dough called beignets. The city's lifestyle, "It's a killer," says the city coroner, Dr. Frank Minyear, who also says autopsies reveal clogging of the arteries in people not yet 30.[1]

This is a sorry picture, and in my opinion, inch-by-inch suicide.

NUTRITIONAL HEALTH

In the area of nutritional health, there are some things we know for sure and some things we do not know for sure, as exemplified by widely varying dieting advice. We do know that there is a need to reduce the intake of fats and simple sugars, and to increase the intake of complex carbohydrates, which are starches such as rice, whole grains, beans, and pasta. These are complex carbohydrates that take longer to digest, thus they release their energy gradually, not all at once as simple carbohydrates such as white flour and refined sugar.

Proteins are necessary in that they build, maintain, and repair muscle tissue. Proteins, however, are not stored in the body as proteins. Therefore, there's a need for some protein every day. Fats and sugars can be stored.

It is relatively easy to tell you what not to eat; it is not so easy to tell you specifically what to eat. I'm not a medical doctor, nor a nutritionist. I am, however, extremely interested in my health and in your health too.

To keep up with nutrition and common medical problems, I subscribe to four monthly medical reports written by medical doctors. These journals often mention the importance of a good breakfast, but never outlined what that was. I developed my own regular breakfast consisting of one soft-boiled egg, buttered toast, a glass of orange juice, and a tall glass of milk. This was prior to the reports on cholesterol clogging arteries. However, once the cholesterol concept hit the press, I immediately dropped my delicious breakfast and switched to a big bowl of oatmeal spiced with lots of plump raisins, bolstered by three tablespoons of wheat germ, and a quarter cup of sunflower seeds. I still included the glasses of orange juice and milk.

I continued this breakfast for several years. I felt good, happy, but . . . soon I read another report. Sure enough, Dr. William Campbell Douglass, editor of the report *Second Opinion*, reported studies to show that eggs and buttered toast are very healthy, in fact, important to good health.

So, what was I to do? I decided to fall back on the common sense advice given by experienced people and philosophers: "Take everything in moderation and nothing in extremes." This ancient wisdom convinced me to combine my two breakfasts, but in smaller portions.

My breakfast routine was re-established and I was happy again. Actually, I was made happier when a recent issue by Dr. Atkins extolled the healthful qualities of wheat germ. He said:

> *"Wheat germ is the source of the oil from which we derive octacosanol. Athletes have noticed marked improvement in physical performance after taking 6 mg a day. A variety of studies confirm that octacosanol can boost muscular strength (including that of the heart), quicken reaction time, and increase muscular endurance."*[2]

You may be wondering why I'm going so deeply into the breakfast meal. Well, breakfast is vitally important, as Jane Brody, a nutritionist who is widely published, says:

> *"Millions of Americans have fallen into a pattern of too-late-for-breakfast, grab-something-for-lunch, eat-a-big-dinner, and nibble-nonstop-until-bedtime. They starve their bodies when they most need fuel and stuff them when they'll be doing nothing more strenuous than flipping the TV dial or pages of a book. When you think about it, the pattern makes no biological sense."*[3]

To follow up Jane Brody's statement, I put forth this paragraph in my book, *How to Study in College*:

> *"The simplest way to put some sense back into your eating routine is by beginning each day with breakfast. Breakfast stokes your body's furnace so you have energy to burn for the rest of the day. Lunch and dinner simply throw a few coals on the fire; breakfast gets that fire burning."*[4]

How About Lunch And Dinner?

What's better, meat or carbohydrates? What to eat for maximum energy and endurance has always been an important question for athletes. Back in the fighting days of Dempsey and Tunney, a big steak dinner before a fight was always the way to go.

WERE THEY RIGHT?

Modern research says "yes." Researchers found that "carb loading" of bread, pasta, potatoes, fruit, and juices did not increase performance. For example, a South African study showed that cyclists on a low 7% carbohydrate diet could pedal twice as long as cyclists on a high 74% carbohydrate diet. Also, a University of New York study confirmed that athletes on a meat diet "performed much better than those on a high carb diet."

ASIDE FROM THE ENERGY AND ENDURANCE FACTORS, HOW ABOUT THE HEART?

Here's the latest: "New research finds that cutting fat levels much below the typical American diet probably won't lower the risk of heart disease for the majority of adults, and it might even increase the hazard for some."[5]

One example regarding the carb-fats question is the diet-story about Bill Walton, the professional basketball player, who was so plagued by constant line fractures of his bones that he had to stop playing basketball. But, once he changed his diet from high carb to eating "some real meat with some fat on it," he made a remarkable recovery.[6]

A second example involves Conchita Martinez, former Wimbledon champion, who hired trainer-nutritionist Tom Tolt to rebuild her body. Tolt redesigned her fitness regimen and replaced pasta with meat. Conchita went on to beat No. 2 seed Lindsay Davenport in the Australian Open; but, was defeated by No. 1 Martina Hingis in the finals.[7]

At this specific juncture, the sports page featuring the Winter Olympics was in front of me and, by chance, I read about cross-country skiing, which is my personal favorite sport. A headline popped out:

USA Lags Behind Cross-country Powers

You see that in the technique of the Norwegians. They are absolutely perfect, start to finish. Every stride is absolutely on, and when you have that, you don't get as tired with each hill.

The Norwegians also do carbohydrate-loading by eating lots of grytte, a type of oatmeal porridge.[8]

A Final Word

What's better? The Norwegians bet on carbohydrates and won. Bill Walton and Conchita Martinez bet on meat and both found proteins better than carbohydrates. So, who's right? Maybe both are. It seems to me that the body needs both the proteins and the carbohydrates, so why not combine them and have the best of both worlds. That's what I do with my breakfast. I recommend and vote for the combination.

Eight Glasses of Water

Yes, I know. Sounds like a lot of water. But, break it down into four stages: two glasses when you get up in the morning, two before lunch, two at mid-afternoon, and two just before dinner. According to Fereydoon Batmanghelidj, M.D.,

> *Every function inside the body is regulated by and depends on water. The brain is 85% water. Approximately 75% of your total body weight is also water. Water must be available to carry vital elements like oxygen, hormones, and chemical messengers to all parts of the body. When I talk about water, I mean just water. Not tea, coffee, sodas, or other fluids.*[9]

Back in 1979, in Ayatollah Khomeini's revolutionary Iran, the doctor was "sardine-packed" in the Evin prison with about 9,000 others who had had contact with Westerners. The doctor's crime was that he graduated from St. Mary's Hospital Medical School in London. It didn't matter that he came back to his country to aid his people.

One night he was awakened by the cries of an inmate in excruciating stomach pain. He was suffering from peptic ulcer disease. Having no medicine, the doctor gave him two full glasses of water.

> *Then the miracle occurred! His pain disappeared in minutes. I knew I had witnessed a healing power of water that I had not been taught in medical school. To my surprise and delight, I found water could treat and cure more diseases than any medication I know about.*[10]

After reading this account, I hope it is with you as it is with me: I'm sold on the health-maintaining qualities of water. Henceforth, it's eight glasses of water every day.

Margarine, Butter, & Olive Oil

Avoid margarine. Butter is much better. Olive oil is best. A study done by the Harvard School of Public Health shows that "ordinary stick margarine and foods baked and fried with shortening and other kinds of hardened vegetable oil" contribute to heart disease by raising the blood levels with bad cholesterol.[11] This cholesterol partially clogs the blood vessels. Why is this clogging so very bad? Here's why. Did you know, when put end to end, there are approximately several miles of arteries, veins, and tiny capillaries in your body? Just think. Your heart, about the size of a clenched fist, has to pump and push a pipeline of blood by beating every several seconds, day after day, year after year. A partially clogged pipeline makes it all the tougher.[12]

Dr. Douglass, editor of *Second Opinion*, says there's nothing wrong with good old-fashioned butter. Use it instead of margarine every time. And for your salads, use extra virgin olive oil, which is so good for the heart he recommends taking at least one tablespoon daily. Dr. Douglass points out, "In Spain, with the highest consumption of olive oil, there is a death rate from heart disease of less than a third that of Finland, where they consume practically no olive oil."[13]

To help your heart, always eat healthy meals. Eat loads of fruit and vegetables, drink eight glasses of water (beer and soft drinks don't count), get out every day for a walk or slow jog, breathe fresh air deeply, get plenty of sleep, and absolutely no smoking or chewing. This will help to keep you out of the statistics that show ten out of every 24 deaths annually are due to heart disease.[14]

Smoking

When asked how long it takes for a cigarette to harm you, one California doctor answered, "About three seconds." In just three seconds, your heart begins to pound an extra fifteen beats per minute, raising your blood pressure about twenty points. And that's just the short-term effect.[15]

What about secondhand smoke? Exposure to secondhand smoke speeds up the clogging or hardening of the arteries and can lead to heart attacks, strokes, and kidney failure. Worse yet, the study found that even decades after a smoker has quit or has inhaled secondhand smoke, the arteries continue to harden or narrow at a much faster rate than they would otherwise. In other words, smoking damage is permanent and irreversible. These are the findings published in the *Journal of the American Medical Association*.[16]

Look what secondhand smoke did to children who lived with two or more smokers before age three. These children had an 85% higher risk of middle-ear infections than children not exposed, a Canadian study shows.[17]

What about cigars? DON'T! A picture on *Tennis* magazine's cover of the world-famous tennis champion, Pete Sampras, raised a storm of protests. The trouble was that the picture showed him smoking a cigar. There has been a renaissance of cigar smoking recently, especially by young adults. A troubling aspect of this new social phenomenon is that people who take up smoking cigars in place of cigarettes tend to inhale more heavily than those who have never smoked. Thus, people who switch from cigarettes to cigars with the thought that they will be safer are deluding themselves. Cigar smoke, no less than cigarette smoke, delivers substantial amounts of nicotine and carbon monoxide into the body. It can also cause cancer. Consider, too, that the people around you will be passively exposed to your smoke.

Self-discipline

At the first meeting of the squad, I make each man stand proud and tall by laying it on the line, telling them, *it's up to you.* They know from the veterans that if anyone misses practice because of a paper to write or an exam to study for, he'll sit on the bench whether he's a super-star or sub.

The desire to play and the privilege of playing are so great that the men discipline themselves by sloughing off all social activities and concentrating only on academics and athletics. They know there's no time for anything else.

I have thirty years of records showing that my student-athletes earned *higher* academic grades *during* the playing season than during the off-season, and that's without exception. I think that's a perfect example that success comes through self-discipline.

BOB CULLEN, former *Head Coach Cornell Lightweight Football*

Vocabulary: Building a Background

Definition: ac-cu-mu-late—1. To gather or pile up; amass.

> WORD HISTORY: *Accumulate*—When, in conversation, a man refers to the accumulating of a fortune as "making his pile," he is using exactly the same figurative language as that which first suggested the word *accumulate*. *Cumulus* is Latin for "a heap or pile," and *cumulare* means "to pile up." With the prefix ad, meaning "to," we have accumulare, "to heap together," which is the source of our English word accumulate. Note: The prefix *ad*, meaning "to," changes to *ac* to fit phonetically to the root word, *cumulu*, whose initial consonant is *c*.

Words in Context

Directions: Make a light check mark (✓) alongside one of the two words (choices) that most nearly expresses the meaning of the italicized word in the episodes. (Answers are given on p. 126.) Excerpts reprinted courtesy of *SPORTS ILLUSTRATED*. Copyright ©, Time Inc. All rights reserved.

The 1997 World Series: Cleveland Indians vs Florida Marlins. Not until two men were out in the 11th inning, and six minutes had passed since midnight, did the 1997 season end. It did so when shortstop Edgar Renteria gave Florida its first World Series championship with a line drive that *flicked* off the glove of righthander pitcher Charles Nagy and into center field, a single that sent second baseman Craig Counsell bounding happily home with the winning run.

8. that *flicked* off   struck hard   struck lightly

The 1997 World Series: When Cleveland second baseman Tony Fernandez muffed a grounder in the 11th inning to make the winning run possible (the error put Craig Counsell safely on base), Fernandez took his place in October *infamy* alongside Fred Snodgrass, the New York Giants' center fielder whose dropped ball in 1912 allowed the Boston Red Sox to win in their last at bat.

9. in October *infamy*   disgrace   glory

The 1997 World Series: Game 4 was played in 18 degree windchill with flurries that made Cleveland's Jacobs Field resemble a *gargantuan version* of those snow globes you can buy at a *knick-knack* shop.

10. a *gargantuan* version   gaudy   large
11. a gargantuan *version*   poem   form
12. a *knick-knack* shop   trinket   sports

NOTES

[1] Tony Horwitz, *The Wall Street Journal*, 23 February 1998: A1.

[2] Dr. Robert Atkins, *Health Revelations*, Vol. V, No. 2, February 1998: 8. (Robert C. Atkins, M.D., Lee Clifford, Agora Health Publishing. 410-895-7900 or FAX 410-895-7901)

[3] Jane E. Brody, *Jane Brody's Good Food Book* (New York: Norton, 1985) 187.

[4] Walter Pauk, *How to Study in College*, 6th ed. (Boston: Houghton Mifflin Co., 1987) 61.

[5] Information taken from the Associated Press in the *Sunday News-Press*, Fort Myers, FL, 15 February 1998: 1.

[6] William Campbell Douglass, M.D., *Second Opinion*, Vol. VIII, January 1998: 7.

[7] Doug Smith, *USA TODAY*, 30 January 1998: 6C.

[8] Gary Mihoces, *USA TODAY*, 20 February 1998: 6E.

[9] Fereydoon Batmanghelidj, M.D., *"Breakthrough Medical Discovery"* letter, March 1998: 2.

[10] Fereydoon Batmanghelidj, M.D., *"Breakthrough Medical Discovery"* letter, March 1998: 3.

[11] William Campbell Douglass, M.D., *Second Opinion*, Vol. VIII, No. 2, February 1998: 2-4.

[12] *Alternative Medicine Digest*, Issue 20: 64-70.

[13] *Alternative Medicine Digest*, Issue 20: 64-70.

[14] William Campbell Douglass, M.D., *Second Opinion*, Vol. VIII, No. 2, February 1998: 2-4.

[15] Walter Pauk, *How to Study in College*, 6th ed. (Boston: Houghton Mifflin Co., 1987) 65.

[16] Robert Langreth, *The Wall Street Journal*, 14 January 1998: A3 and A8.

[17] Steve Sternberg, *USA TODAY*, 11 February 1998: 8B.

3
PLANNING YOUR TIME

Dost thou love life? Then do not squander time, for time is the stuff life is made of.
   –Benjamin Franklin

WHY TIME FLIES.   Most of us waste time so routinely that we aren't even aware of it. That's because the way we use (or abuse) time is largely a matter of habit.

MAKE A SCHEDULE.   It's not kid's stuff. After thirty years of lecturing to business executives, I found that almost 100% of them carried in their shirt pockets a file card generally called, "Things-to-do-Today Card."

WHAT EXECUTIVES SAY.   One executive, a Yale graduate, characterized the pocket schedule by saying, "I used it in college and I'm using it now. It frees my mind. Knowing that I'll not forget the things I have to do, I can concentrate more fully on each task I do. Furthermore, I get a psychological kick out of drawing a line through each item completed."

SCHEDULES AFFECT DAILY LIFE.   How we perform in our work affects our overall attitude toward life. A student athlete who is overwhelmed by academic work will often feel overwhelmed by life in general, consequently, not performing in the sports arena to full potential. Because a time schedule presents a rational approach to your work, it is bound to improve your general disposition.

SCHEDULES

Boiling it down realistically, you need three types of schedules.

1. THE PERMANENT SCHEDULE: This one doesn't change throughout the semester. In the time blocks, fill in your daily classes and labs; include breakfast, lunch, and dinner; regular athletic practice sessions; and sleep—getting-up time as well as regular going-to-bed time.

2. THE WEEKLY SCHEDULE: Put big X's in the blocks to represent the permanent schedule. Then add by filling in the blocks when the team will be traveling and playing. Important: plan your study strategy for the week; for example, when to start writing a research paper. Fill in other blanks with "study," "exercise," "movies," and so forth.

3. THE DAILY SCHEDULE: As already explained, the big plus of the daily schedule is that it can be carried almost anywhere. All it really consists of is a 3x5 card or slip of paper. Another advantage is that it isolates the activities of a single day. This can help to make the day more manageable.

    Daily schedule, the workhorse: Write out the next day's schedule just before going to bed. The great value is that as you *think* your way through the next day's activities, you embed each time not only on paper but also in your mind. You've psyched yourself for the next day's work, and the chances are great that, in the morning, you'll hit the floor running.

SCHEDULING GUIDELINES

Here are eight tips to keep in mind.

1. ELIMINATE "DEAD HOURS." One of the very first goals of a time schedule is to eliminate the "dead hours," such as the half-hour trip to "just pick up a newspaper," or the "coffee break" that nearly takes an hour. These are the "little things" that really add up to rob you of your precious time.

2. USE DAYLIGHT HOURS. Business, work, and society are programmed to work during the day and sleep during the night; so you better adjust to it. Here's an interesting fact. Research shows that productivity is cut in half

when night time comes. In other words, four hours of work after midnight is equivalent to two hours of work during the day.

3. RECITATION CLASSES AND LECTURE CLASSES. In classes in which you might be called on to recite, schedule a study period just before such a class to give yourself time to review your textbook assignment. For lecture classes, schedule a study period directly after this class to study the notes while they are still fresh in mind.

4. DISCOVER HOW LONG TO STUDY. At first, allow a reasonable amount of time for your subjects; then, by experience, notice whether you've allotted too much time or too little for each subject. Adjust as you go along so that your future schedules are realistic.

5. ALLOW SUFFICIENT TIME FOR SLEEP. Very recent research from the Sleep Center in California found that most college students are "sleep starved." That's why they fall asleep in class, in the library, and at their desks. Its data show that students in their late teens and early twenties need as much as 8 to 9 1/2 hours of sleep every night. This sleep, they found, must come during the night. Why at night? Because at night your pineal gland, a small cone-shaped organ in the brain, secretes at least five times more melatonin in your blood than during the day. And, what's so important about melatonin? It not only helps you to sleep sounder, but also helps to prevent tumors since it stimulates our tissues to destroy oxidants, chemical pollutants that produce cancer.[1]

Those who get sufficient night-time sleep, these research studies show, live longer than those who don't. You can see why, because in addition to the tumor-fighting quality of melatonin, deep sleep recharges the entire body, repairs tissue, and most important, rejuvenates the central nervous system.

It seems that Ben Franklin, even way back then, had it right when he said, *"Early to bed and early to rise makes a man healthy, wealthy, and wise."*

6. ALLOW SUFFICIENT TIME FOR MEALS AND EXERCISE. Remember, you have to start the day with a good breakfast; so, obey the alarm clock. The pace you set at breakfast will affect the whole day. A rushed breakfast will set a frantic tone, and learning is inefficient in such an atmosphere. Allow time to enjoy lunch and dinner. These are some of the pleasures in life. Meals also allow you to relax and socialize a bit. Remember too, your health is at stake.

7. DIVIDE AND CONQUER. Assignments, especially big assignments, are best handled when you divide them into bit-sized chunks or blocks. This way, when you finish off each piece you'll have a feeling of accomplishment, which should spur you on.

8. DON'T PACK YOUR SCHEDULE TOO TIGHTLY. Remember that buses don't always run on time, pencils need sharpening, papers get lost in the shuffle, games go into overtime. In other words, give yourself some breathing time for life's little inconveniences. If you don't, one minor setback could cause your entire schedule to collapse.

HOW TO STUDY ON THE RUN

You can't buy nor make more time; but, you can *find* more time. How? By using minutes and even hours that were previously wasted. Here's how to find more time.

1. WALKING TO A CLASSROOM. Before leaving your room, glance at your lecture notes, then, as you walk toward the classroom building, recite to yourself the previous lecture. Recall and recite as much of it as you can. In this way, you will link the previous lecture with today's lecture, like this: ⦶⦶⦶ thus, each lecture will not be an isolated link, like this — ◯◯◯◯.

2. WALKING FROM A CLASSROOM. Upon walking from a classroom, where you listened and took notes, make it a habit to recall and recite all the main points of the lecture you just heard.

3. REFLECTION. What's reflection? It's thinking about one important idea heard in class or read in your textbook. Your objective is to try to take the idea a step further by asking yourself: Why is this idea important? How does it relate to other subjects? Does it affect the way I see the world? What would be the next logical step beyond this idea? In other words, just think and speculate and mentally play with the idea. As Professor Hans Bethe, Cornell's Nobel prize winner said, "Every person can become a creative person, if he would just spend some part of every day thinking and reflecting."

4. WAITING TIME. When standing in line or sitting in an outer office, whip out a thin stack of file cards with facts from your classroom lecture or your textbooks. Study and memorize them.

5. POCKET DICTIONARY. Carry one. Just open it up and read it. No one thing will help you more in life than speaking easily and correctly.

COMMENT—Reciting your lectures as you walk, reflecting on ideas wherever you are, going through pocket file cards while waiting—I don't know of any more sure and powerful way to master a subject.

STUDY ON ROAD TRIPS

Road trips are fun, but they do take big blocks of time. As a result, you're faced with a Sunday evening mountain of work. But, you can reduce this mountain by following these tips:

1. INSTRUCTOR. Always pause and let the instructor know that you'll be missing the next class. Ask for any handouts and suggestions for making up or catching up. You'll establish yourself as a caring student, which could help you greatly in a pinch.

2. FRIENDS. Remind your friends-in-class to take complete notes, because you'll need all the help you can get to capture what was said.

3. LIMITED OBJECTIVES. For the bus or plane trip, don't overload yourself. If you do, very little will get done. Rather, carve out a few important parts of a subject or two. For example, take along your lecture notes for a subject. Using the Cornell System (see Chapter 8), you can quietly recall and recite the notes. You can take along one textbook: read a paragraph, stop to think about it, then go back to underline the main points and write a few cue words and phrases in the margin. Figure out for yourself what type of work-on-the-bus or plane is best for you. But, by all means, use this precious time for study.

4. THE GAME. I predict that if you study while traveling, you'll do better in the athletic game. You'll feel in control of things. Studying while traveling takes active, positive thinking, as well as concentration. These attitudes and actions will be carried over to the game itself.

Time-Saving Tips

Here are ten more time-saving tips which should help to keep you on the right track.

1. GUARD AGAINST PARKINSON'S LAW. Parkinson's Law says, "A job will expand to fill the space allotted for it." In other words, if you set off two hours to do a one hour assignment, you will most probably take the whole two hours to do it. So, guard against this law by making a hard and realistic estimate of how long it should take you to complete every assignment. Once you have budgeted your time in this way, stick to it.

    However, we are all different, so assess yourself. If you don't work well under pressure, provide a little cushion of time. On the other hand, if you work better with a bit of fire under you, adopt the tactic of Duke Ellington, the great jazz musician who said, "Without a deadline, I can't finish nothin'."

2. DON'T LOOK BACK. The finish line is straight ahead, not behind you. So, don't waste precious time by rehashing the past.

3. SHOW SOME COURAGE. Have the courage to be yourself. As you know, most people do not use time wisely; so, don't be delayed by such a group. Set out on your own to manage your time properly.

4. CONCENTRATE YOUR TIME AND EFFORTS. The best way to do this is to set priorities for yourself. R. James Steffen, a management consultant and recognized expert on time management, recommends using the ultimate time organizer. According to Steffen, "By that, I mean identifying the most important thing to be done now and then having the freedom to perform the task with total abandon. Forget everything else and concentrate wholeheartedly on that activity."

5. TAKE FREQUENT STUDY BREAKS. Study breaks do not use up precious time. Only prolonged study breaks do. Brief but frequent breaks actually increase your overall productivity by discouraging "study burnout." Guard against long breaks by following your time schedule and using self-discipline.

6. OBEY THE ALARM CLOCK. There's no sense kidding yourself. Playing games with the alarm clock first thing in the morning can set the tone for your entire day. Start the day out right by making your feet hit the floor as soon as your alarm goes off. It isn't easy, I know; but, as soon as you're fully awake, you'll be glad you did.

7. BEAT THAT SLEEPY FEELING. Don't give in by taking a nap. Almost everyone has periods of drowsiness during the day. If you feel drowsy at the same time every day, plan something active, such as: (a) If you need some research data, go to the library where you'll be active looking up references and books. (b) If you have rough notes for a paper, type them. (c) Take your lecture notes and pace the floor as you recite from them. (d) If you must finish a chapter, pace the floor while reading aloud. Above all, don't sit there trying to read. You'll surely cave in. Finally, don't resort to caffeine, which will alter your body chemistry.

8. WRITE NOTES TO YOURSELF. Don't clog your mind with thoughts. Put them on paper so you don't waste time wracking your brain to recall them.

9. USE A MONTH-AT-A-GLANCE CALENDAR. With a day-by-day calendar, tomorrow's responsibilities can be out of sight and out of mind. In order to organize your time, you need the big picture. That means weeks and months, not just days.

10. GET A HEAD START. Here's how: (a) Get your class schedule set before classes begin. That way, you can use your time schedule right away. (b) Buy your textbooks immediately so you won't be caught empty-handed. (c) Make certain you know where all your classes will be held. (d) Make a strong resolution from the start never to miss a class while on campus.

> *If You Can't Manage Time*
>
> . . . then, life will be a series of crises. But, manage time by scheduling classes, tests, recreation, nights off, tutors, even spending money, and you'll be a success.
>
> TOM MILLER, former *Head Coach, University of Colorado Basketball*

> Throughout my coaching career, I have always tried to impress upon my student athletes the importance of balancing "the three S's"—school, soccer, and social life. If one can maintain a healthy balance of each, you will most likely be a successful individual.
>
> BECKY BURLEIGH, *Head Women's Soccer Coach, University of Florida*

NOTES

[1] Dr. Marcus Laux. "Sleep Starved Students" *Naturally Well II*, No. 10 (October 1995): 4.

Vocabulary: Building a Background

Definition: acumen—Quickness, accuracy, and keenness of judgment or insight.

> WORD HISTORY: A keen mind may be likened to a sharp knife, which penetrates easily and quickly. For clean-cut action, both the knife and the mind must be sharp. So it is natural that, when a word was needed to denote the quality of keen, penetrating thought, the Latin word for "sharpness" was borrowed. The Latin *acuere* means "to sharpen" and *acumen* means "sharpness." English borrowed *acumen* and used it figuratively for sharpness of the mind.

Words in Context

Directions: Make a light check mark (✓) alongside one of the two words (choices) that most nearly expresses the meaning of the italicized word in the episodes. (Answers are given on p. 126.) Excerpts reprinted courtesy of *SPORTS ILLUSTRATED*. Copyright ©, Time Inc. All rights reserved.

Even so, Colorado Rockies manager Don Baylor was *disheartened* that Andres Galarraga didn't try harder to stay with the team that *revitalized* his career.

13. was *disheartened*	hesitant	disappointed
14. *revitalized* his career	revived	reversed

Dave Wannstedt's fifth season as Chicago Bears' coach has been an *unmitigated* disaster, and he may not be around to coach a sixth, but give him credit for staying the course. At the helm of a team with *meager* talent, Wannstedt has *refrained* from panicking and has worked hard to keep the Bears from unraveling.

15. an *unmitigated* disaster	noticeable	absolute
16. with *meager* talent	scant	major
17. has *refrained* from	restrained	indulged himself

Bryan Cox drew a crucial 15-yard penalty for yanking off his helmet while arguing with an official. A more *incendiary* coach—Dave Wannstedt's *predecessor* Mike Ditka, for example—would've given Bryan Cox a few dozen *decibels* worth of grief, as many Chicago Bears players did on the sideline. But Dave Wannstedt calmly told Cox to cool it for a series, then sent him back into the game.

18. a more *incendiary* coach	inflammatory	incompetent
19. Wannstedt's *predecessor*	person after	person before
20. a few dozen *decibels*	measure sound	measure embarrassment

SEIZE THE MOMENT

I believe that only one person in a thousand knows the trick of really living in the present. Most of us spend 59 minutes an hour living in the past with regret for lost joys, or shame for things badly done (both utterly useless and weakening) or in a future which we either long for or dread. The only way to live is to accept each minute as an unrepeatable miracle, which is exactly what it is—a miracle and unrepeatable.   –Storm Jameson

4
IMPROVING YOUR CONCENTRATION

High jumpers . . . are given two minutes to prepare for each attempt. Former world record holder Dwight Stones is noted for spending that time in a virtual trance state, arousing himself with mental images of making the approach and soaring over the bar. He concentrates so fixedly on these images that his head actually bobs—you can see it from the side-lines—as he "watches" his own imaginary form through every galloping step of his approach run to come. Sometimes, he says, his image knocks off the crossbar—and he will not start an actual jump until he sees his ghost form succeed.

Source: John Jerome, *The Sweet Spot in Time*,
New York, Summit Books

CONCENTRATION

We've all seen the power of concentration; for example, the clean-as-a-whistle foul shot, under tremendous last second pressure. On the other hand, a perfect pass in football, but, the receiver turns his attention too soon to the on-rushing tackler.

With concentration we succeed; without it we fail. So it is in sports; so it is in academics.

EXTERNAL DISTRACTIONS

Avoid distractions. Just as a pass receiver can be distracted by things around him, so a studying-student can be distracted by things around him. You must find your quiet study spot. It can mean the difference between great success and dismal failure.

THE LIBRARY.   The library is probably your best bet. Yet, there are varying degrees of distraction even there; so, look around within the library to find your spot.

YOUR ROOM.   If you are in a noisy living quarter, make up your mind right from the beginning to move to the library. With conversations in the hall and music next door, there's no sense trying to shut out the noise mentally while your eyes read and re-read the same paragraph without any meaning going beyond the eyeball.

MUSIC AND STUDYING.   Let's face it. Music is a distraction. Research shows that the mind cannot entertain two separate thoughts simultaneously. It's one or the other. So, when you recognize the music, you're not recognizing the meaning of the words in the book you're studying. Furthermore, if you work to shut out the music from your consciousness, then you are using physical and nervous energy to shut out something that you have the power to eliminate in the first place. So, if you like music, listen to it during your break; but, not while trying to study.

INTERNAL DISTRACTIONS

There are distractions that come from the inside rather than the outside. Daydreaming and worry are the two biggest offenders.

DAYDREAMING.   Daydreaming is a habit which can be stopped by raw self-discipline. Don't permit this breaker-of-concentration to get the upper hand. As you already know, daydreaming is a vicious time waster too.

WORRY.	Personal problems (and everybody has them) can do more than any other distraction to disrupt your concentration. Although these problems should not be left to solve themselves, there is a time and place for everything. If something bothers you while you are studying, write it down quickly and tell yourself that you will cope with it as soon as you have finished studying.
BIG PROBLEMS.	If the problem is so great that it can't be ignored, put down your pencil and take action right away. If you cannot solve the problem yourself, get the help of someone you trust. The sooner the problem is out of the way, the sooner you can go back to work.

LIGHTING

Good lighting is absolutely necessary. Nothing can give you a dull headache faster, tire your eyes quicker, make taking a nap irresistible, than poor lighting.

GOOD LIGHTING.	To eliminate glare and shadows, you need two light sources. The general source is from a ceiling or floor lamp. The specific source is from your desk lamp.
INCANDESCENT BULBS.	If you use a bulb-type lamp, make sure it has a full shade on it. A partially shaded bulb or an unshaded bulb can reduce the clarity of your vision by more than 80% in just three hours.
THE BEST DESK LAMP.	I used a double-tube fluorescent lamp of the drafter's type for over forty years. Fluorescent light comes closer to daylight than an incandescent bulb.
	All fluorescent bulbs flicker; but, when you have a pair of tubes, they are synchronized, so you have continuous, even light. Several years ago, the Dazor Company came out with a three-bulb fluorescent desk lamp. It's a beauty! Nothing is too expensive for the good of your eyes.

INDIRECT LIGHTING. Last year I switched to indirect lighting. The light from the incandescent bulb is reflected upward to a metal domed top, which then reflects the light downward onto my desk. For my older eyes, this indirect lighting is kinder and less harsh, minimizing glare.

GENERAL HEALTH & CONCENTRATION

General health can affect your energy and concentration. As an athlete, you get enough exercise; but, you should pay special attention to your diet and sleep.

DIET.

We've already talked about food and nutrition in Chapter 2; but, I want to emphasize the absolute importance of a good breakfast. Combine protein (eggs or fortified milk) for long-lasting blood sugar with carbohydrates (whole wheat bread or cereal such as oatmeal) for clean-burning energy.

SLEEP.

Again, in your late teens and early twenties, you need from 8 to 9 1/2 hours of sleep every night. To sleep sounder, avoid caffeine completely throughout the day. Don't take naps. When sleepy, do a few minutes of exercises. It works!

SLEEP CYCLE.

Establish a strict routine. Don't vary it. Your body runs on a cycle of waking and sleeping. Frequent changes disrupt you both mentally and physically. That's what "jet lag" is: a disruption of the sleep cycle. You can cause it without flying.

CAN'T SLEEP?

If you're already in bed and can't sleep, don't worry about it. Dr. Rudolf Hess, Swiss mental specialist and Nobel Prize winner, offers the following advice:

". . . resign yourself to it, arrange your limbs comfortably and enjoy the feeling of their relaxed heaviness. Occupy your mind with pleasant thoughts and memories, without worrying about the passage of time. Then, sleep, too, will come."

Subject is "Boring"?

Here are four ways to make "boring" subjects more interesting.

1. Small group sessions. Get together with two or three other students (teammates perhaps) and discuss each assignment in your "boring" subject. Don't go along for a free ride. Make sure that you and every member of your group does his or her homework.

2. Tutoring. Don't put off getting help until exam time. By then it may be too late. Go to your coach, friend, or college tutoring service to get help.

3. Alternative textbooks. If the required text isn't getting through to you, go to the library and hunt for an alternative text that makes more sense. Chapter for chapter, use the alternate text in conjunction with the required text.

4. Workbooks and programmed instructional materials. These have step-by-step instruction, which should help you to understand your subject easier and better.

Concentration Techniques

Five techniques for maintaining concentration:

1. Think positively—Look upon studying as an opportunity to learn instead of an unpleasant task.

2. Be well-equipped—Keep on hand a dictionary, textbooks, calculator, clock, note cards, rubber bands, glue, paper, erasers, and clips. Use a stand designed to hold your book open in a tilted position. It frees your hands to underline and write. Also it takes away from the strain of a bent head and neck.

3. The no-room technique—By giving 100% attention to the material in your textbook, you fill your mind and consciousness completely. Then, when a stray thought tries to break in, there will be no room. So, in this way, your concentration will remain unbroken.

4. CHECKMARK TECHNIQUE—Whenever you find yourself not concentrating, put a checkmark on a blank piece of paper. The mere act of making a mark will remind you to get back to work. You'll make fewer and fewer checkmarks as time goes on.

5. THE GREAT PENCIL TECHNIQUE—It's the simplest and most effective technique I know. I've "sold" it to hundreds of business executives, as well as students: whenever you are working to learn, study with a pencil in hand. And use it! If you are reading a textbook, stop after every few paragraphs and briefly jot down the author's key points. If you can't come up with any, you probably haven't been concentrating enough. Go back and re-read the passages until you do. Activity is the key toward promoting concentration. The pencil provides the activity!

Concentration Gets the Job Done!

VOCABULARY: BUILDING A BACKGROUND

Definition: as-sas-sin—1. One who murders by surprise attack, especially one who carries out a plot to kill a prominent person.

> WORD HISTORY: *Assassin*—In eleventh-century Persia, a secret order was founded among the Ismaili, a Mohammedan sect, by Hassan ben Sabbah. The absolute head of this order was the Old Man of the Mountain. Its members indulged in the use of the Oriental drug, hashish, and, when under its influence, in the fanatical practice of secret murder. This terrible organization spread terror over Persia, Syria, and Asia Minor for nearly two centuries. The murderous drinker of hashish came to be called *hashshas*, "one who has drunk of the hashish," and from that origin comes our English word *assassin*.

WORDS IN CONTEXT

Directions: Make a light check mark (✓) alongside one of the two words (choices) that most nearly expresses the meaning of the italicized word in the episodes. (Answers are given on p. 126.) Excerpts reprinted courtesy of *SPORTS ILLUSTRATED*. Copyright ©, Time Inc. All rights reserved.

Brian Schottenheimer, the son of Kansas City Chiefs coach Marty Schottenheimer, is in his first year as the St. Louis Rams' offensive *intern*, a job that pays $9,600 annually. He has the following statement taped on the wall of his Rams Park *cubicle*: "The best kind of pride is that which *compels* a man to do his very best when no one is watching."

21. offensive *intern*	trainee	assistant coach
22. Rams Park *cubicle*	small office	square office
23. *compels* a man	prepares	drives

New England Patriots vs Jacksonville Jaguars: Drew Bledsoe, the Patriots' quarterback, called every play during that series, and his *execution* was flawless. He finished 26 for 35 for 234 yards and two touchdowns, and for the third *consecutive* game he did not throw an interception.

24. his *execution* was flawless	exhibition	performance
25. third *consecutive* game	successive	championship

Despite leading the New England Patriots with 57 catches this year, Ben Coates, a great pass receiver, in five games, has had three or fewer catches. Last week Ben Coates said, "It has been kind of *frustrating* watching this offense because I am *capable* of making so many more plays."

26. kind of *frustrating*	gratifying	discouraging
27. *capable* of making	able	inept

Discipline seems to be a word that turns a lot of athletes off, but I think it is the key to survival for most student-athletes. True, practices, weight-room work, and travel to and from games are very time-consuming, but let's be honest: it's not a violation of an NCAA rule to take books on a road trip.

I think it's laughable that a football player or basketball player can't budget a few hours of study a day on his own to get a degree. It takes some discipline and a little sacrifice to juggle athletics and academics, but what the athlete has to gain is so great. Too many of them don't realize it.

A school owes its student-athletes an education, but the student-athlete owes himself the **guts** *to put priorities straight and get it.*

> DAVID DUPREE, *Sports Writer USA TODAY; University of Washington*

5

STRENGTHENING YOUR MEMORY

Forgetting is often embarrassingly swift; especially, when names are forgotten minutes after an introduction. The frequent excuse is, "I just have a poor memory for names." Yet, there are those who seem to have a bear-trap memory, not only for names, but also for figures and facts as well. What's their secret? What techniques do they use? In this chapter we'll explore the problem of forgetting and come up with ways to help ensure remembering.

MEMORY

What do we know about the memory? Some ancients thought that the memory was located in the heart; but, of course, everyone now knows it is in the brain.

A more interesting question is this: how are names, facts, and figures *recorded* in the brain? The early psychologists thought that grooves, like those on a record, were made by the blood's coursing through the brain cells. This idea, however, was soon discarded. The answer now is that molecular changes are made in the brain cells. These changes are analogous to the molecular changes and arrangements made on a cassette tape.

To better understand the memory, let's get acquainted with the short-term and long-term memories.

SHORT-TERM MEMORY

Research over the years shows that almost everything we see, hear, and read enters the short-term memory first. This information is like a stream that flows into our consciousness and out the other side. If dammed up in the memory, the jingle of every commercial you ever saw or heard would still be floating around in your head.

So, if there's some fact in this flowing stream that you want to keep, you better grab it before it is jettisoned for good.

LONG-TERM MEMORY

The long-term memory is like a separate compartment with no doors in it. So, even if you grab a piece of interesting information that flows through your short-term memory, you cannot force it into the long-term memory either by choice or by brute strength. The only way to transfer information is by *thinking* through the compartment walls of the long-term memory.

This special type of thinking is a process called *Reciting*, which psychologists say is, as a memory technique, the most powerful of all.

RECITING

When you find a fact that you want to remember, you must write it out on paper, study it for a few minutes to gain full understanding, then, without looking at the paper, recite aloud the idea in your own words. It is this reciting in your own words that makes you genuinely think. And it is this variety of thinking that enables the idea to gain entrance into the long-term memory.

We will be using this technique of reciting in the chapters on taking lecture notes as well as the textbook reading chapter.

Words & Pictures

We all know that the brain is divided into two sections: the left hemisphere and the right hemisphere. Psychologists, however, found an interesting fact: the left side processes and stores verbal information (words), while the right side processes and stores visual information (pictures). So, when we memorize a fact using words only, we're making use of only half our brain power. But, when we draw a picture of a fact and use words to describe this fact, we put both sides of the brain to work.

We will also be using this technique in the chapters on taking lecture notes and textbook reading.

Clustering (Categorizing)

Whenever you have a list of names, places, or facts to remember, take time to reorganize them into groups in which they best fit or belong. Why? Because grouping will help you to memorize more items in a shorter amount of time. For example, below are twenty names listed in a non-organized way. It would take you many minutes to memorize perfectly all these individual names.

Steffi Graf	Martina Hingis	Venus Williams	Chris Evert
Mark Messier	Wayne Gretsky	Eric Lindros	Mario Lemieux
Jerry Rice	Troy Aikman	Cordell Stewart	Brett Favre
Ken Griffey	Cal Ripken	Mo Vaughn	Andres Galarraga
Monica Seles	Paul Kariya	Reggie White	Gary Sheffield

But, if you first put these names into their natural groups, the time to memorize them would be drastically shortened, perhaps 10 to 1 in time.

Tennis	Hockey	Football	Baseball
Steffi Graf	Mark Messier	Jerry Rice	Ken Griffey
Martina Hingus	Wayne Gretzky	Troy Aikman	Cal Ripken
Venus Williams	Eric Lindors	Cordell Stewart	Mo Vaughn
Chris Evert	Mario Lemieux	Brett Favre	Andres Galarraga
Monica Seles	Paul Kariya	Reggie White	Gary Sheffield

CONSOLIDATION

You should know about consolidation. Consolidation is the time that it takes information to sink in. In order to remember information effectively, the mind must be given some sinking-in time. A remarkable story reveals that facts are not memorized immediately.

> *A mountain climber fell and hit his head on a rock. When he regained conscious-ness, to no one's surprise, he couldn't remember the fall. What startled everyone is the fact that he couldn't remember anything that had happened during the last fifteen minutes before his accident. His mind had not been given enough time to consolidate his memories before he hit his head!*

Knowing that your memory needs consolidation time should affect your study habits. First, it supports the idea of recitation. By reciting what you learn, you hold the information in mind long enough for it to be consolidated. Second, it supports the practice of brief, but frequent breaks during a study session. These breaks not only give you a needed rest, they also allow your mind some time to consolidate what you have just learned.

REMEMBERING NAMES

Keep in mind this game-plan:

1. When an introduction is about to be made, immediately get ready. Think to yourself, "Here comes a name. I'm going to give my full attention to the person and listen keenly for the name."

2. Make sure you get the name straight immediately. For example, if you are introduced to Ronald Raines, immediately repeat the name by saying, perhaps, "Nice to meet you Ronald Raines. By the way, is your last name spelled *Rains* or *Raines*?" He might answer, "Neither, It's Raynes." In any event, you have achieved your goal.

3. During the conversation, say the name a few times. This type of "recitation" will help to get a correct, crisp, clear image of the name into your long-term memory.

4. Also, during the conversation, mentally spell the name a few times, all the while making a connection between the face and the name.

5. Ask about his job or hobbies. Again, try to connect the name with the job or hobbies.

6. Be interested. It is said that we remember the names of those in whom we're genuinely interested. The others, we forget. So, be interested!

FINAL WORD—The method just outlined for remembering names is really no different from the method of remembering facts.

1. Stay on top by studying every night. Don't get behind!
2. Create an interest in every course. For example, physics was dull until I applied the laws of physics to various angles of a basketball shot, then I picked up not only interest, but also a high grade.
3. *Use* techniques in study skills books. You must have blind faith that they will organize you and change your habits. If you have faith, these skills will pull you through academically.

BRAD NADBORNE, former *Assistant Coach, University of Colorado Basketball*

Vocabulary: Building a Background

> Definition: sal-a-ry—Fixed compensation for services, paid to a person on a regular basis.

> **WORD HISTORY:** *salary*—originally, salt money. Roman soldiers, as a part of their pay, drew a special allowance for the purchase of salt, not always so easily obtained in ancient times as now. The allowance "for salt" was called *salarium*, from *sal*, "salt." The word was later used to mean "pension." Latin *salarium* was borrowed in English as *salary*, "fixed regular wages," but used in connection with civilian workers only, not soldiers. A soldier draws his "pay," not a *salary*!

Words in Context

Directions: Make a light check mark (✓) alongside one of the two words (choices) that most nearly expresses the meaning of the italicized word in the episodes. (Answers are given on p. 126.) Excerpts reprinted courtesy of *SPORTS ILLUSTRATED*. Copyright ©, Time Inc. All rights reserved.

After 57 years at Grambling, Eddie Robinson retires as the NCAA's winningest coach. Robinson was always a master *motivator*, *theatrical* and *preachy*, wholly *manipulative*. His speeches, which he practiced in front of his wife, Doris, were *legendary* and *fraught* with outsized emotion. "He'd cry before a big game," remembers Doug Williams, the former Grambling and NFL quarterback, now coach at Morehouse College and the leading candidate to replace Robinson.

28. a master *motivator*	disciplinarian	stimulator
29. *theatrical*	insensitive	dramatic
30. *preachy*	unrelenting	instructive
31. wholly *manipulative*	convincing	controlling
32. speeches were *legendary*	genuine	remembered
33. *fraught* with emotion	filled	heightened

Coach Eddie Robinson now embarks on a *typical monologue* that, as he has aged, has gotten increasingly *circuitous*, looping here and there. But, just like that, he arrives at the point and delivers it fiercely: "You're losing a little bit of what Grambling was."

34. a *typical* monologue	standard	unusual
35. a typical *monologue*	conversation	lecture
36. increasingly *circuitous*	direct	roundabout

6

BUILDING YOUR
VOCABULARY

LEARNING THE HISTORY OF WORDS

Language is a wonderful thing. Each word has a meaning and a part to play in communications. It is only when we learn the life history of a word that the full realization that each word has an ancestry comes over us.

Back of almost every word in the English language there is a "life story" that will come to many as a fascinating revelation. Our words have come to us from a multitude of sources. Some of them have lived for thousands of years and have played their parts in many lands and many civilizations. They may record ancient superstitions. They may be monuments to customs dating back to classical antiquity. They may reveal our ancestors' manners and beliefs, shrouded in the mists of ancient history. Words that you use today may have been the slang of Roman soldiers twenty centuries ago or the lingo of Malay savages. They may have been used by an Athenian poet or by an Anglo-Saxon farmer.[1]

What is needed for all learning is interest, a sense of excitement about words, a sense of wonder, and a feeling of pleasure—these are the essential ingredients in vocabulary development.   –Lee Deighton

INTEREST.   Professor Deighton is 100% correct. If you have an interest in words, then each word that you explore will impart excitement, wonder, and pleasure. "Great!" you might say, "but, how do you acquire such an interest?"

HERE'S HOW.   Once you find out that behind almost every word in the English language there is a life story, words will henceforth take on a living, interesting quality.

FOR EXAMPLE.   Take the word, *agony*, which is not only pictured here but also explained, and you will see what I mean when I say that almost every word in the English language has a fascinating history. Later, in your reading, whenever you run across such a word, it will be like meeting a well-known friend. The word's meaning will be rich—far beyond a mere dictionary synonym.

Agony

"By permission. From *Picturesque Word Origins* ©1933 by Merriam-Webster, Incorporated (formerly G. & C. Merriam Company)."

Agony: from an ancient athletic meet

It is strange that a word which denotes anguish and intolerable pain should have its origin in a festive sport event; yet that is the case with agony. In ancient Greece, agon was a public assembly, especially one for public games and athletic contests. Agonia was the contest or struggle for the prize. From the meaning "a struggle for victory in the games," agonia gradually broadened to mean any physical struggle, an activity fraught with difficulty or pain, and then mental anguish of mind, then the throes of death, and hence an extreme suffering of body or mind.

REFERENCE.   The picture and explanation of the word *agony* came from a book titled *Picturesque Word Origins*, published by Merriam-Webster. Unfortunately, the book is no longer in print, but you might find a copy in your library. There are other books devoted to word origins. Look for them in your library. Most, however, are not illustrated. I have included a list of books covering word origin, both in- and out-of-print, at the end of this chapter for you to use for further study.

Finally, throughout *The American Heritage Dictionary of the English Language*, third edition, published by Houghton Mifflin Company, are word histories, making it a perfect book for browsing.

NON-ILLUS-
TRATED
WORDS.
Though illustrations help, they are not essential to spark interest in words. Take *neatsfoot oil* for example:

> Anyone who takes good care of a baseball glove has heard of *neatsfoot oil*. Yet, few people know the origin of this trusty oil's name. Despite what you may think, neatsfoot has nothing to do with the fact that this popular glove lubricant can also be used to keep a pair of leather shoes looking nice. The key to the mystery of neatsfoot oil lies in a meaning for *neat* that we no longer use. Up until the late nineteenth century, the word *neat* referred to any animal of the bovine family, that is, cows and oxen. Not surprisingly, the oil that ballplayers swear by is made by boiling the shin bones and feet of cattle.

VOCABULARY
AND SUCCESS.
No matter what your goals are, you'll need a good vocabulary for success.

ACADEMIC
SUCCESS.
In one study, a college found that the students who improved most in vocabulary during their freshman year averaged three or four places nearer the top of their class in academic standing during the sophomore year.

BUSINESS
SUCCESS.
The Human Engineering Laboratory found an almost perfect correlation between high vocabulary scores and success at the top executive levels.

VOCABULARY AND THINKING. Psychologists agree that thinking is silent speech. In other words, when you think you do the same thing you do when you speak, only silently. In fact, studies have shown that thinking is accompanied by slight movements of the lips and other speech muscles. This means that if your vocabulary is limited or imprecise, your thinking will be as well.

VOCABULARY BUILDING

The most important tool for vocabulary building is a dictionary. I have always owned and depended on three of them.

New Webster's Vest Pocket Dictionary – True to its name, it can fit into a vest pocket. Its small size makes it easy to carry around. What a perfect book to read to fill in minutes that might otherwise be wasted. For only a very small sum, you can buy one from Dennison Manufacturing Company, Framingham, MA 01701.

Desk dictionary: Merriam-Webster's Collegiate – Always have it at your fingertips when studying. You'll need it for definitions and pronunciations. The Greek and Latin roots, prefixes, and suffixes, alongside most words, will help you to understand and remember them better.

Unabridged dictionary – This is the big volume you'll find in the library. By using an unabridged dictionary, you'll get a rather full story of any word you look up. In the desk type, you must sacrifice part of the story.

Some computers have dictionaries too, as does the Internet.

VOCABULARY CARDS

I believe the most practical way to increase your vocabulary is by writing the words you want to master on file cards.

FRONT OF THE CARD. At the top, write the full sentence in which you encountered the word. Underline the word so that it will stand out. To master any word, you must know how to pronounce it; so, divide the word into syllables and include all of the marks that will indicate the accented syllable, as well as the marks that indicate long and short vowels.

For example, the word *sodium* (sō'-dē-əm) would have the straight, long diacritical marks over the vowels ō and ē to indicate that these vowels have a sound just like the names of the letters; that is, an ō would be sounded as the word *Oh* and the ē sounded like the e in the word *see*.

The diacritical mark ˘ signifies a short vowel like the *a* in *pat* (păt) and the *e* in *pet* (pĕt). Look for the Pronunciation Key in the front pages of your dictionary for how to read the diacritical marks, which will help you to pronounce words correctly.

BACK OF THE CARD. On the very top, write the prefix and root that pertain to the word's origin. This is just for your information. No need to memorize them. Then select the definition that defines the word on the front of the card. Also, select a second definition.

Figure 6.1 – VOCABULARY CARD

Front   Back

| Coach Robinson embarks on a typical <u>mono-logue</u> that has gotten increasingly circuitous.

mŏn'-o-logue
(mŏn'-ə-log) | mono (Greek) = one; single; alone
logos (Greek) = word; speech

*1. A long speech made by one person.
  2. A continuous series of jokes or comic stories delivered by one comedian. |

ROOTS AND PREFIXES.

Knowing a word's derivation can often tell you things about the word that you might not have learned from its definitions. For example, most of us know that a sophomore is a second-year student. But if you look at the derivation, you'll find that it comes from two Greek words, *sophos*, meaning wise and clever, and *moros*, meaning foolish or silly. Apparently, the Greeks felt second-year students were both educated and naive. Thus, they were wise fools. If you remember your sophomore year in high school or college, you'll see there's some truth in this.

USING THE CARDS.

Carry about a dozen of these cards around with you so you can review them whenever you have a bit of spare time. Grab one card at a time and look at the front side. Read the sentence completely, pronounce the word correctly, and then define it. Try to use your own words instead of the dictionary language.

After you've defined the word to the best of your ability, flip the card over and check your definition with the dictionary definition. If correct, move to the next card. If not, flip to the front side and put a dot in the upper right-hand corner. This dot will remind you that you missed on a previous try. If a card gets three or more dots, it's time to give that word some extra attention.

After mastering one stack, put them into the file box and grab another small stack. From time to time, you may want to refer to your file box and review those words you've already mastered.

PERSONAL WORDS.

The words selected so far are words you're interested in, because they suit and fit your personality. These words will be learned fast and well.

TEXTBOOK AND LECTURE WORDS.

The words and terms from textbooks and lectures have to be learned cold whether you like it or not. It would be a great mistake not to learn the precise meaning of such words. You might lose a few points on an exam or perhaps even jeopardize your overall understanding of the course.

Follow the same procedure that you used for your personal words. Although you may not be as interested in these words at first, once you have an understanding of their precise meanings, the words and the class from which they came may become more exciting to you.

BUILDING A PRECISE VOCABULARY. Be especially watchful for words that sound somewhat alike. Here's a good example of what I mean.

A Switch-hitting frog?

Baseball's great Yogi Berra is notorious for his misuse of words that sound somewhat alike. Here's what he said about teammate Mickey Mantle: "Mantle can hit just as good right-handed as he can left-handed. He's just naturally *amphibious*." Of course, *amphibious* means "able to live both on land and in the water." What Yogi meant was *ambidextrous*, which means "able to use both hands equally well." The remark didn't even elicit a croak from Mantle, who by then was quite accustomed to his teammate's unique use of the English language.

EVEN ONE WORD A DAY. Let's end with Dean Trembly's words of wisdom.

The world judges you on your potential when you are young. As you go through your twenties, thirties, and forties, the world looks more and more at how much you know and what you can do. Aptitudes will give you a good start, but it takes vocabulary to keep you going. Don't wait too long to start working with words.

If marooned on a desert island, the one book that would hold your interest for years would be **Webster's New World Dictionary**. *There you'd gain wisdom as you pondered over 200,000 definitions, and knowledge as you reflected upon such up-to-date words as cloning, electronic mail, genetic engineering, cyberspace, Hubbel telescope, and the Mir space station. Then, too, you'd feel pleasure in just plain browsing. You'd be surprised that the word* **yogurt** *was used back in 1625,* **warmonger** *in 1590, and* **marshmallow** *before the 12th century. So, if you're looking for wisdom, knowledge, and pleasure, with the dictionary at your fingertips, you'll find them.*

BOOKS IN PRINT

Ciardi, John, *A Browser's Dictionary and Native's Guide to the Unknown American Language*. Published in 1980. Information and copies: Harper & Row Publishers, Inc., 10 East 53rd St., New York, NY 10022.

Funk, Charles E., *A Hog on Ice, and Other Curious Expressions*. Published in 1948. Information and copies: Harper & Row Publishers, Inc., 10 East 53rd St., New York, NY 10022.

Holt, Alfred H., *Phrase and Word Origins*. Published in 1961. Information and copies: Dover Publication, Inc., 31 East Second St., Mineola, NY 11501.

Hook, J. N., *The Grand Panjandrum*. Published in 1980. Information and copies: Macmillan Publishing Co., Inc., 866 Third Avenue, New York, NY 10022.

Maleska, Eugene T., *A Pleasure in Words*. Published in 1981. Information and copies: Simon and Schuster, 1230 Avenue of the Americas, New York, NY 10020.

Mathews, Mitford M., *American Words*. Published in 1959 and again in 1976. Information and copies: Philomel Books, 200 Madison Avenue, New York, NY 10016.

Word Mysteries & Histories. Published in 1980. Information and copies: Houghton Mifflin Co., 222 Berkeley St., Boston, MA 02116.

OUT-OF-PRINT BOOKS

Ernst, Margaret S., *In a Word*. Published in 1939 by Alfred A. Knopf, New York.

Picturesque Word Origins. Published in 1933 by G. & C. Merriam Company, Springfield, MA.

NOTES

[1] From *Interesting Origins of English Words*, (G. & C. Merriam Co., Publishers of the Merriam-Webster Dictionaries, 1959).

VOCABULARY: BUILDING A BACKGROUND

Definition: bon-fire—A large outdoor fire.

WORD HISTORY: *Bonfire*—a fire of bones. In the Middle Ages, funeral pyres for human bodies were a necessity in emergencies of war or pestilence. *Bonefires* (fires of bones) they were called. Later, when the custom of burning heretics at the stake became common, *bonefires* was the name applied to the pyres of these victims. Finally, its meaning was extended to open-air fires for public celebrations or sports— but by this time in the less gruesome spelling of *bonfire*, which today is a comparatively harmless word despite its grim history.

WORDS IN CONTEXT

Directions: Make a light check mark (✓) alongside one of the two words (choices) that most nearly expresses the meaning of the italicized word in the episodes. (Answers are given on p. 126.) Excerpts reprinted courtesy of *SPORTS ILLUSTRATED*. Copyright ©, Time Inc. All rights reserved.

Fennis Dembo, a native of San Antonio, and his unforgettable *appellation*, is a burly 6'6" forward with a *penchant* for *flamboyance* and a *predilection* for chaps and Stetsons. Dembo, as a junior, helped the Wyoming Cowboys reach the Sweet 16 of the NCAA basketball tournament. His most memorable game came in the second round, in which he *torched* UCLA for 41 points while *bombarding* the Bruins' Reggie Miller with verbal *shrapnel*.

37.	unforgettable *appellation*	name	supporters
38.	a *penchant*	dislike	inclination
39.	for *flamboyance*	showiness	sloppiness
40.	a *predilection*	preference	aversion
41.	he *torched* UCLA	burned	salvaged
42.	while *bombarding*	surrounding	attacking
43.	with verbal *shrapnel*	fragments	insults

Perhaps more *ominous*, the five-time champion Chicago Bulls' *aura* of *invincibility* had *evaporated*. Losing to the Cleveland Cavaliers by 21 points? Could a squad that still included Michael Jordan have *deteriorated* into just another team?

44.	perhaps more *ominous*	sinister	impressive
45.	Bulls' *aura* of	record	feeling
46.	aura of *invincibility*	unbeatable	insecurity
47.	had *evaporated*	risen	disappeared
48.	*deteriorated* into	melted	neutralized

The pursuit of academic and athletic excellence is something I value as one of the most rewarding experiences in life. Being a successful student athlete requires preparing as diligently for the classroom as for the competitive playing field.

JOHN HACKWORTH, *Head Men's Soccer Coach, University of South Florida*

7
READING AND STUDYING YOUR TEXTBOOK

The hardest job in college is reading the textbook. Why? Because the ideas therein are usually new to us; and worse still, worded in formal language. Often, after plodding through a paragraph and understanding each separate word, we still find it difficult to answer the question: "What did the author say?"

TEXTBOOK ASSIGNMENTS

"Read Chapter 5," for example, is the way assignments are usually given. But, don't take the instructor at his/her word; because, he/she really means more than *read*. He actually means, *read, understand, and remember the principles, ideas, facts, and details of Chapter 5*. Now, that's a tall order! And, you better understand and remember, because he/she is going to check up on you with quizzes and exams.

READING TO UNDERSTAND

Here's how:

1. NOTICE THE CHAPTER'S TITLE. Read the title of the chapter and think, for a minute, about its meaning. Then, again, for another minute, speculate on what the chapter might be about.

2. FLIP THROUGH THE PAGES. Flip each page, read the dark print (the captions), and pause to notice pictures and graphs. Finally, read the last portion (paragraph or section) that summarizes the chapter. Oh, yes! You should have also read the first paragraph. Though this flipping and spot reading doesn't take much time or effort, they accomplish a lot. This action acquaints you with the chapter, and also gets you started.

3. GO BACK TO THE BEGINNING OF THE CHAPTER. And read, without pausing, about three, four, or five paragraphs—enough to find a good stopping place. Then, go back, and after reading carefully the first paragraph, stop to answer this question: "What did the author say?" If no answer is forthcoming, you must read and reread the paragraph until it makes sense and you can explain it in your own words.

    Don't become discouraged. This re-reading will not go on forever. With practice, you'll soon learn to crack the meaning of a paragraph at the first reading. It's similar to practicing in sports. But to forge ahead without understanding paragraph after paragraph is to invite academic disaster.

4. UNDERLINING. Do *no* underlining until after you have explained the paragraph in your own words. Now that you understand the paragraph, you will know where the key words, phrases, and sentences are located. Underline only these. Be stingy with your underlinings, because, later, when you have to review many chapters for a quiz or exam, you want your eyes to dart directly to the key words, phrases, and sentences, without having to read the whole paragraph over again. In other words, the hard and precise work you do now will set you up for an effective and efficient review later—especially when time just before an exam is so precious.

5. MAKING NOTES IN THE MARGIN. Make short notes in the margin of the page. Here's why. Having just explained the paragraph in your own words, and having just underlined, you most probably reached a high level of under-

standing. It is crucial, at this point, to capture this understanding in the form of notes in the margins. If not captured, much will be forgotten. Furthermore, these notes in the margin will be of tremendous help to you when you review for a quiz or exam. So, the more you do now, the easier and better the studying, learning, and remembering will be later.

6. CUE WORDS AND PHRASES. The words and phrases in the margins have one more *vital* role, perhaps the most important role, to play in the process of learning and remembering. These words and phrases will act as cue words. For example, in dramatic plays, cue words remind actors of their lines. In the margin of your textbook, cue words should remind you of facts and ideas underlined on the textbook page.

7. USING CUE WORDS AND PHRASES. Place a blank sheet over the textbook page, exposing only the notes in the margin. Then, taking a cue from each word or phrase, recite aloud, in your own words and from memory, the facts and ideas hidden from view which are on the textbook page.

8. RECITING MAKES FOR A POWERFUL MEMORY. Reciting takes ideas from the desktop of your short-term memory and stores them away in the filing cabinet of your long-term memory. Once the facts and ideas are in the filing cabinet, you have a good chance of retrieving them later when needed. Left in your short-term memory, the facts and ideas are almost certain to be misplaced or irretrievably lost in a matter of days or hours, and often in a matter of minutes. Many studies show dramatic improvement in remembering where reciting is part of the study routine.

TAKING SEPARATE NOTES

Rather than depending on the underlinings and notations in the margins of a textbook, some students prefer to make separate notes in a notebook. There are some advantages.

ADVANTAGES

1. Making your own notes is an active process, keeping you alert and thinking.
2. Reading a textbook paragraph forces you to come to a definite interpretation before writing it down in your notebook.

3. Writing out the interpretation is similar to the writing you'd be doing in taking an exam; so, you'd be getting practice.
4. There's something appealing about having all your notes on a few sheets of paper, instead of notations scattered in the margins of twenty or so textbook pages.
5. These compact notes would make studying for a quiz or exam easier.

DISADVANTAGE

Separate notetaking can be time consuming, especially if you include too many details. If you do, you'll be almost rewriting the textbook. Worse still, if you spend so much time writing, you'll have less time studying.

TAKING NOTES

If you decide to take separate notes, here are some guidelines:

1. Use the Cornell Notetaking System (explained in Chapter 8).
2. Write your notes in full sentences and in your own words, just as you would in an exam.
3. Finish reading the paragraph or section before taking notes.
4. Be extremely selective. Pick out only the essentials from each paragraph. If you try to remember too much, you may not remember very much.
5. Be swift. Read, go back for a mini-overview, and then take notes. Be fast and efficient without being careless.
6. Strive for neatness. Your notes may make sense today, but will they still be readable at the end of the semester?
7. Don't forget visual materials. Treat them as you would other important facts and ideas by reviewing and reciting them.

OUTSIDE READING

These collateral materials are usually assigned to provide you with a viewpoint or special material that your textbook may lack. If your course clearly has a core textbook, then there is little reason to study the collateral materials as carefully as the primary text. However, this does not mean that these special assignments may be skipped. They must still be read, understood, and remembered. Here are five basic steps for approaching a collateral assignment.

1. FIGURE OUT WHY THE BOOK WAS ASSIGNED. Have a rough idea of what you're supposed to get out of the reading before you begin to read it.
2. READ THE PREFACE. By now you should know the value of this part of the book. Pay close attention to why the collateral assignment is different from your text.
3. LOOK OVER THE TABLE OF CONTENTS. Notice how the chapter titles differ from those in your text. Read the information that does not seem to be covered in your primary textbook.
4. READ THE SUMMARY PARAGRAPHS. Located at the end of each chapter, there's a good chance that these distilled bits of writing will give you a clue as to the book's particular "angle."
5. DON'T LEAVE THE BOOK WITH ONLY VAGUE NOTIONS. Make sure that you can say something definite about it in class or on an upcoming exam. Be ready to answer any broad or general questions about its main issues, the author's approach, or the similarities and differences between it and your primary text. Think big instead of getting bogged down by details.

SPEED READING

Will a course in speed reading help me with my reading? The answer is a definite *NO!* Having researched, lectured, written, and taught speed reading over many years, I can say with a sense of certainty that speed reading is a hoax. Don't waste your time and money on such a course. The only course that can help you is a course in study skills. And, this book is your study skills course.

VOCABULARY: BUILDING A BACKGROUND

Definition: hum-ble—Marked by modesty in behavior, attitude, or spirit; not arrogant or prideful.

> WORD HISTORY: *Humble*—literally, on the ground. *Humus* in Latin means "earth," "ground," and the derived adjective *humilis* means "on the ground," "low." Latin *humilis* became French *humble*, which was taken into English. *Humble* is now more commonly figurative: "thinking lowly of one's self."

WORDS IN CONTEXT

Directions: Make a light check mark (✓) alongside one of the two words (choices) that most nearly expresses the meaning of the italicized word in the episodes. (Answers are given on p. 126.) Excerpts reprinted courtesy of *SPORTS ILLUSTRATED*. Copyright ©, Time Inc. All rights reserved.

Chicago Bulls' assistant coach Tex Winter, the architect of the triangle, says Scottie Pippen's absence isn't solely to blame for the Bulls' *abysmal* shooting.

49. *abysmal* shooting	accurate	hopeless

The Heisman is an institution *replete* with many things: a brand-name visibility, an *austere* Saturday-evening television show, and finally, a black-tie presentation dinner two nights later.

50. *replete* with	proud	filled
51. *austere* TV show	somber	lengthy

Jeff Bagwell was part of the Houston Astros' Killer Breeze offense that *flailed* and failed against the Atlanta Braves' *parsimonious* pitching. When Houston's *formidable* trio of Craig Biggio, Derek Bell and Jeff Bagwell went 2 for 37 against Atlanta last week, the Killer B's were instantly *ridiculed* as the Killer Breeze.

52. that *flailed*	suffered	thrashed
53. *parsimonious* pitching	stingy	generous
54. *formidable* trio	awesome	consecutive
55. instantly *ridiculed*	ribbed	hailed

8
TAKING LECTURE NOTES

Getting information from a textbook takes a lot of time and hard work. Even then, you can't be sure that you have understood completely and chosen wisely. In contrast, getting information from a lecture is duck soup. The lecturer has already chosen what's important. The difficult ideas and principles are explained, illustrated, and diagrammed. Furthermore, you can ask questions and get answers. What an opportunity! What a bonanza! And yet, what I often see when I pass a lecture room are sleepy heads and reclining pencils.

AGGRESSIVE NOTETAKER.
Be an aggressive notetaker. Work hard to concentrate and extract everything valuable out of a lecture.

DON'T SKIP LECTURES.
When not on the road, attend lectures faithfully. But, when on the road, consider pairing up with another athlete who plays a sport at a different time of year than you do. Such a person would better understand the importance of taking clear and complete notes for you. Furthermore, you can return the favor when your athlete-friend is on the road.

WHY TAKE NOTES?
Because of forgetting. Recent research shows that an average student remembers about 50 percent of a ten minute lecture when tested immediately, and only 25 percent when tested forty-eight hours later. Four weeks later, just before an exam, the percentage, obviously, might be around 10 to 15 percent. Forgetting is swift, massive, sure, and unforgiving.

YOUR OBJECTIVE?
Your objective is to capture on paper the lecturer's ideas so that you can carry them back to your room for careful study.

THE CORNELL NOTETAKING SYSTEM

The Cornell format helps you to organize your notes. This System remains one of the most effective and widely used notetaking systems yet devised (See Figure 8.1).

THE NOTETAKING COLUMN

Write your notes in the wide column. Begin writing immediately and keep on writing throughout the lecture. But, don't take the lecture word by word like a secretary; rather, capture the lecturer's "points" in telegraphic sentences. If the lecture is moving too fast, skip some space so you can fill in later by either asking the lecturer or your friends. Remember that your objective is to take sufficient notes so that you can recite the lecture from your notes directly after the lecture or during that day's evening.

Figure 8.1 THE CORNELL FORMAT

2 1/2" **Cue Column**	6" **Notetaking Column**
Reduce ideas & facts to concise words & phrases.	Record the lecture as fully and as meaningfully as possible. Use telegraphic sentences.

TELEGRAPHIC SENTENCE
Here's an example of a full sentence and a telegraphic sentence.

FULL SENTENCE: A top speed of over 70 miles per hour makes the cheetah the world's fastest animal.

TELEGRAPHIC: Cheetah–world's fastest animal–70mph

GENERAL RULE: Get rid of as much as possible of a sentence without destroying its meaning.

Notetaking Tips

1. Get to class a little early and sit where you can easily see and hear everything the lecturer does and says. Begin taking notes from the first word and don't stop until the lecture is over.

2. In taking notes, use your own words or the lecturer's words. It doesn't matter. Do what's easiest and fastest.

3. Be alert for clues. "This is a common pitfall," "This is important," or "You'll see this later," might be uttered by the lecturer.

4. Use symbols (asterisks, arrows, etc.) to indicate ideas that the lecturer emphasizes.

5. Always record the lecturer's examples and things written on the board.

6. Don't close shop too early. The end of the lecture often contains important conclusions and summaries.

7. Don't stop to think about some point being made. If you do, you'll miss the next point or two. By capturing all the points, you can do your thinking later when you read your lecture notes.

8. If the lecture is going too fast, raise your hand and politely ask to slow it down.

9. Use only those abbreviations that you can write easily and later translate without any trouble.

10. Avoid formal outlining. Use indentations and skipping of spaces to show units of thought. Indent the details a bit farther so you can see and know them at a glance.

11. Do not type or rewrite your notes. This wastes time. So, do it right the first time! Make yourself write legibly. You can, if you try.

12. Use the modified print-writing style (See Figure 8.2).

13. Don't use shorthand, because you'll have to waste time transcribing.

14. Don't use cassettes, because you can't then read the lecture. Why spend another fifty minutes listening to the locked-up facts, especially if you don't need them all.

15. Use a large loose-leaf notebook. This enables you to take sheets out and insert classroom handouts. Don't use spiral-bound notebooks.

16. Write on only one side of a sheet.

17. Look over the notes of the previous lecture to connect it with the upcoming one.

18. Always write on the top of your first sheet, the course name, course number, lecturer's name, date, and day.

19. It's hard to know what's important or relatively unimportant; so, take everything and sort out later. The basic rule: take notes; judge later.

20. Pre-reading the textbook chapter will help you to anticipate the lecturer's points and to follow the development of the topic.

STUDYING YOUR NOTES

Immediately after the lecture, or the first opportunity you have, fill in any gaps that you may have in your notes.

CUE COLUMN

By filling in the gaps and reading over your notes, you will have recaptured the whole lecture. So, now is the ideal time to fill in the cue column. Notice the cue column in Figure 8.2. In the cue column, write the key words and phrases that will give you a "handle" to the complete facts and ideas that the cue words stand for.

Figure 8.2 THE CORNELL NOTETAKING SYSTEM IN ACTION

	Sept. 8, 1998 – Econ. 201–Prof. Keay
Crash of 1929	A. The crash of 1929 –stock market
	1. Dow Jones Industrial average
Dow Jones	-low 153 (1927) to high 381 (Oct. '29)
153-381	-149% gain in 2 yrs.
Ex. RCA 500%	Ex. RCA gained 500% in 1928
	2. Cause Fed. Res. lowered int. rates
Cause low int. rates	cheap money gives econ. false
	stimulus inflation
Speculators borrowed	3. Speculators borrowed to play
	stock market.
Sucked in public	4. Boom sucked in 1000's of amateurs
	5. Warning signs of bust:
Warning signs	-too much optimism
-optimism	Ex. Prof. Fisher (Yale) "stock prices
	have reached permanently a
	high plateau."
	Ex. Pres. Coolidge stocks "cheap
	at current prices"
Brokers called in loans	6. Crash Oct. '29 brokers demanded
	payment of margin-loans
	-investors dumped stock to raise cash
	-crash brokers jumping out of windows
Dow down 89%	7. Oct. '29 (top) - July '32 (bottom)
-bottom 7/32	Dow down 89%
	-biggest crash in Am. financial history
	8. Wiped out speculators and businesses

USING THE CUE COLUMN

Once you have written in the key words in the cue column, you're ready to do the most important step of *reciting*. Here's how: take the first page of your notes and cover all except the cue column with a piece of blank paper. Then, use the key words as cues to remind you of what your notes say. Then, recite your notes aloud, using your own words. After reciting, uncover your notes to make sure that your reciting was correct.

Psychologists have proven time after time that reciting is the most powerful technique for combating forgetting.

LISTENING SKILLS

One way to improve your listening skills is to eliminate the bad habits which affect the way you listen. Ralph G. Nichols, an internationally-known expert on listening, has pinpointed ten bad listening habits. On the following chart (Figure 8.3), I have adapted Ralph Nichols' work by listing not only the poor habits, but also, what the good habits should be.

Figure 8.3 IMPROVE YOUR LISTENING SKILLS

Poor Listeners	*Good Listeners*
1. Call a subject dull.	1. Find an interesting angle.
2. Criticize speaker's looks, dress, manner, etc.	2. Never mind the speaker. Look for ideas delivered.
3. Overreact with emotions.	3. Listen with their minds.
4. Listen for facts only, losing the "big picture."	4. Listen for the overall facts and details.
5. Outlining: so concerned with format, miss theme.	5. Adjust notetaking to fit speaker's pattern.
6. Fake attention. Pretend listening.	6. Give genuine attention.
7. Yield to distractions. Ex.—noises, coughs, etc.	7. Shut out distractions by concentrating on ideas.
8. Hang on to the simplest parts of the lecture.	8. Unafraid of tough, technical or complex ideas.
9. See red at words like fascism, communism, evolution, etc., so stop listening.	9. Take such words as signals to see speaker's prejudices.
10. Between sentences and pauses, daydream or brood.	10. Between sentences and pauses, review speaker's points.

Vocabulary: Building a Background

Definition: ex-ag-ger-ate—To represent as greater than is actually the case; overstate.

> WORD HISTORY: *Exaggerate*—literally, to heap up. When one tells a story with a good bit of exaggeration, he is, in the colloquial phrase, "piling it on," which comes very close to translating the word *exaggerate*. This is derived from Latin *exaggerare*, "to heap up," an intensive form of *aggerare*, "to bring to," "bring on," from *ad*, "to," and *gerere*, "to bear," "bring." Its English meaning was also "to heap up," "to accumulate," but this sense has disappeared, leaving the figurative one, "to enlarge beyond bounds or truth," "to overstate."

Words in Context

Directions: Make a light check mark (✓) alongside one of the two words (choices) that most nearly expresses the meaning of the italicized word in the episodes. (Answers are given on p. 126.) Excerpts reprinted courtesy of *SPORTS ILLUSTRATED*. Copyright ©, Time Inc. All rights reserved.

San Francisco Giants' left fielder, Barry Bonds, is one of the few players who could appreciate Gary Sheffield's *subtle* yet *devastating* contribution to the Florida Marlin's Division Series victory. Sheffield reached base 10 times in 14 plate appearances. Five of those times he got on with a walk.

56. Sheffield's *subtle*   quiet   obvious
57. *devastating* contribution   average   overwhelming

However, with the regular season winding down, Gary Sheffield experienced an *epiphany* of sorts by calling upon advice he'd received from Barry Bonds, the left fielder of the San Francisco Giants, earlier in the summer. "Stay patient. When they finally challenge you, make them pay."

58. experienced an *epiphany*   hindsight   vision

Bobsledding: Billy Fiske quickly made a cohesive team out of his *diverse* crew of Gray and Eagan, and after the four Lake Placid runs were completed, Fiske again was Olympic champion. The victory was *historic* for more than one reason: Billy Fiske and Clifford (Tippy) Gray had each won their second gold medals. And Eddie Eagan created a record that still stands: He's the only athlete, male or female, to win gold medals in both Summer and Winter Olympic Games.

59. *diverse* crew   assorted   consolidated
60. victory was *historic*   exciting   outstanding

9
MASTERING YOUR NOTES

Your notes–page after page packed with facts. You must transfer these facts into your memory. Unless you do, they'll do you no good.

THREE WAYS

The three ways that will help to cement your notes in your memory are REVIEW, RECITATION, and REFLECTION.

REVIEWING LECTURE NOTES

Some of these techniques have been mentioned before, but let's consolidate them here, because they're so important.

1. AFTER THE LECTURE. While walking away, make it a habit to recall the main points of the lecture. Don't become discouraged. I guarantee that you'll become better and better at it. Furthermore, you'll enjoy this important scholarly process.

2. CONSOLIDATION. By immediately planting the facts of the lecture in your mind, the important process of consolidation will take place. You'll be giving time for facts to sink deeply into the long-term memory.

3. FILL IN THE BLANK SPACES. Make time to sit down almost immediately after class to fill in the blank spaces while the lecture is still fresh in mind. Also, make any scribbles more legible. Finally, underline or box in the words that contain main ideas.

4. CUE COLUMN. Go back through your notes and extract the key words or phrases that will remind you of each important idea.

RECITING LECTURE NOTES

After you've written the key words for every crucial idea, take a blank piece of paper, cover up the right side of your note page, look at the key word, and recite *aloud* from memory and in your own words, the fact or idea that the key word refers to.

A BONUS STEP – Take an entire lecture's note sheets out of the binder and overlap them so that only the cue columns are exposed. By now, the key words should remind you of the lecture's key ideas. As a result, you should be able to get an idea of the lecture as a whole with a little more than a glance. It helps the memory when you end up with an overview of this sort.

PREVIOUS LECTURES – Reviewing and reciting are important. Pull out your notes from previous lectures once in a while and go through this process.

REVIEWING YOUR TEXTBOOK – The paragraph-by-paragraph reading method is perfect for immediate reviewing. Each time after you've read a paragraph and made notes in the margin, take a minute right away to cover up the text and recite what you have just read.

ADVANTAGES OF IMMEDIATE RECITATION

FOUR ADVANTAGES:

1. Promotes immediate concentration.
2. Forms a sound basis for understanding the next paragraph.
3. Gives your memory time to consolidate what you've just learned.
4. Provides immediate feedback on how you're doing.

RECITING THE TEXTBOOK FACTS – Reciting is the thing! It does the job of putting facts into your memory. Reading is really just the tip of the iceberg when it comes to mastering your textbook efficiently. So, after you've finished reading and marking a chapter, go back, cover up the text, and recite using the key words as your clues.

LATER REVIEW – Later reviews are important for both lecture and textbook notes if you are to make any progress in your war against forgetting. Some of these reviews could take place on the bus or plane while enroute to a game or meet.

REFLECTION

Though this is high-powered stuff, it can be done by anyone who has a strong will and who aggressively wants to rise above the average.

REFLECTION VERSUS REVIEWING

Reviewing deals with the information that is there in black and white, whether it is printed in your textbook or written in your notebook. Reflection deals with information that is between the lines; information and conclusions that you are able to arrive at on your own.

A NOBEL PRIZE WINNER TALKS ABOUT REFLECTION

Professor Hans Bethe, nuclear physicist and Nobel prize winner, had this to say about reflection:

> *There's a world of difference between proficiency and creativity. A student can become proficient by studying his textbooks and lecture notes, but he will never be creative until he attempts to see beyond the facts, tries to leap mentally beyond the given. He must reflect on the facts and ideas, for creativity comes only through reflection.*

QUESTIONS YOU CAN USE FOR REFLECTION

Here are some general questions that should help you to begin reflecting on your lectures and textbook assignments:

1. What is the significance of these facts or ideas?

2. What principle are they based on?

3. What else could they be applied to?

4. How do they fit in with what I already know?

5. What can I see that lies beyond these facts and ideas but is still based upon them?

TAKES A LOT OF TIME? Not at all. What's more, unlike reviewing or reciting, reflection can be done almost anywhere. There's no need for notes or a textbook. All it requires is an inquisitive mind. If you run, swim, or lift weights regularly, reflection is a perfect thing to occupy your mind while you're exercising. You can also reflect when you're walking to and from classes or waiting in a line.

VOCABULARY: BUILDING A BACKGROUND

Definition: par-a-site—1. Biology. An organism that grows, feeds, and is sheltered on or in a different organism while contributing nothing to the survival of its host. 2. One who habitually takes advantage of the generosity of others without making any useful return.

> WORD HISTORY: *Parasite*—eating at the table of another. Among the Greeks and Romans there was a class of men who made themselves welcome at the houses of rich men by providing flattering entertainment, especially at meals. The Greeks called such a man *parasitos*, from *para*, "beside," and *sitos*, "wheat," "grain," or "food." Thus the word meant one "eating beside" another, and hence, one who, without doing useful work himself, manages to be supported by another. Latin borrowed the word as *parasitus*, and English as *parasite*. Its first meaning was close to the original Greek sense, but it came to be applied, in biology, to a plant or animal living in, on, or with some other living organism at whose expense it obtains its food, shelter, or some other advantage.

WORDS IN CONTEXT

Directions: Make a light check mark (✓) alongside one of the two words (choices) that most nearly expresses the meaning of the italicized word in the episodes. (Answers are given on p. 126.) Excerpts reprinted courtesy of *SPORTS ILLUSTRATED*. Copyright ©, Time Inc. All rights reserved.

On the day after the San Francisco Forty-niners opened its season with a 13-6 loss to the Buccaneers in Tampa Bay, Steve Mariucci was still shell-shocked from having experienced the most devastating *debut* since New Coke. That the 42-year old Steve Mariucci, coach of the San Francisco 49ers, shook off his rocky start is a *testament* to his *composure*, *optimism* and sense of humor.

61. devastating *debut*	losing appearance	first appearance
62. is a *testament*	proof	important
63. his *composure*	self-possession	conduct
64. his *optimism*	perfection	hopefulness

"The Sooners of Oklahoma have some great athletes and they play *incredibly* hard, but I think they make a few too many mistakes," the Nebraska Cornhuskers offensive tackle Eric Anderson said last week. "And sometimes they don't play together. Sometimes they seem to have different *agendas* down there."

65. play *incredibly* hard	remarkably	unpredictably
66. different *agendas*	opponents	plans

Pursue your academics by preparing and participating with the same passion as you do your athletics.

SHERRY BEDINGFIELD, *Head Women's Tennis Coach, University of South Florida*

Three things kept me in good academic standing: first, I promised myself that I'd do my homework every night no matter how tired I was; second, as I read my textbook, after every paragraph I'd stop and convert the author's words into my own; and third, it was a matter of personal pride never to give up.

TOM "SATCH" SANDERS, *Associate Director of the Center for the Study of Sports in Society, Northeastern University; Former Head Basketball Coach, Harvard University; Boston Celtics, '60-'73 Eight World-Championship Teams*

10
TAKING TESTS

"When should I start to prepare for the final exam?" The answer: "From the very first day of class!"

◊ ◊ ◊ ◊ ◊ ◊ ◊ ◊ ◊ ◊ ◊ ◊ ◊ ◊ ◊ ◊

A bit of Chinese wisdom tells us, "A journey of a thousand miles begins with the first step." Similarly, the journey to the final exam begins with the first day of class.

FROM THE FIRST DAY OF CLASS

It makes sense! You know from experience that preparation for an important game doesn't begin a few days before the game. No, preparation starts weeks before, with practices, scrimmages, weight-lifting, and so forth. So, why should anyone think that a couple of all-night cramming sessions is all the preparation one needs for an exam?

Even Before the First Day

Here's how to survive academically. Here's how to be super prepared. Buy all your textbooks early. Then, before classes begin, read carefully the preface of each book. Why? To get acquainted with the author. The preface is almost the only place where an author can tell you why he wrote the book, why it is different, what his biases are, and so forth. Once you get to know the author as a real-live person you'll be able to carry on a conversation with him when you study the textbook. For example, when Professor Milton Friedman writes, "There's a direct connection between money growth and inflation," you can now carry on a conversation by asking, "Yeah? What's your proof?" Such a dialogue will make an otherwise dull text alive and interesting.

Remember

Almost all the facts and ideas for which you are responsible come from two sources—the classroom lectures and the textbook assignments. I've already given you the two best systems in the world on how to handle the lectures and the textbooks; so, follow those techniques.

My last pitch: Don't fall behind! Remember the story of the young lad who couldn't break a bundle of sticks? His teacher said, "Untie the string." Then, the boy caught on. He easily snapped the sticks one by one. So it is with your daily assignments. Easy when done day by day; almost impossible when piled up and bunched.

Again: No matter how bruised and tired, do each day's assignments!

Summary Sheets

Here's a system that works wonders, but takes time, effort and discipline to do right. This is an active way to prepare and study for an exam.

Take your stack of classroom notes and systematically select from each sheet the facts and ideas that you believe are the important ones. Write out these facts and ideas on another sheet using the Cornell format (p. 66). Fill in the cue column, too. Now, you should have reduced each day's lecture (four or five sheets) down to not more than one sheet per lecture. These new sheets are now your "master sheets." Your job now, reduced in size, is to recite until you master the facts and ideas on these new sheets.

THE TEXTBOOK

There's no sense rewriting the textbook. So, review your textbook by covering the printed page, exposing only the jottings in the margin, and reciting only those portions of the printed page that you believe are vital. Again, recite until you feel confident that you know your stuff.

CRAMMING

Cramming, like the half-court shot and the onside kick, is a do-or-die situation. Obviously, doing is better than dying; but, this doing had better be done right or you're dead. And, to do it right, you must follow, to a 100% level, these three rules: be extremely *selective* in limiting the facts that you choose to remember; have personal *courage* to resist details and secondary facts; and swear to *work* by reciting until you almost drop. Otherwise, it won't work.

SELECTIVITY

People who cram often fall into the trap of trying to learn too much. In order to succeed you must leave the details behind. Concentrate on essential facts.

FINDING THE FACTS

Start out by skimming each textbook chapter. Put the main ideas on paper that has been ruled in the Cornell format (p. 66). Be sure to write things in your own words. When you have finished going through the textbook, do the same with any lecture notes you might have.

CLEAR YOUR DESK

When the summary sheets are done, push everything else off your desk. Your only job now is to learn every fact on these sheets, cold, and in a limited amount of time.

RECITE

Go through and write in the cue words in the left-hand column that will remind you of the bulk of information in the right. Then, cover all but the cue column and recite out loud and in your own words until you know the stuff backwards and forwards. Of course, you may not remember much of what you've learned after the exam is over; but, your objective is to survive the battle so you can continue the war.

EXAM DAY

SLEEP

Make sure you get nearly eight hours of sleep. If you ever needed a clear mind, it's now. Get up early enough so there'll be no panic. Like Minnesota Fats before a championship pool game, take a good shower, shave, and have a medium breakfast.

A GOOD SEAT

Get there early. That way, you'll be sure of a good seat where the light is good, the blackboard visible, distractions minimal, and away from friends.

REDUCING TENSION

The Doctor's Method was devised to help patients with high blood pressure, but it has also proven to reduce minor tension.

THE DOCTOR'S METHOD FOR REDUCING TENSION

This simple method of relaxation is so inconspicuous that it can be done before, and even during, the exam. It has three steps:

1. Breathe in until your lungs are completely full.
2. Now take a sudden extra gulp of air through your mouth.
3. Let your breath out slowly.

Repeat this procedure several times.

INSTRUCTIONS

Even if the exam sheet is in your hands, listen carefully for last-minute instructions. Next, quickly read the written directions. If there's a question, raise your hand immediately and ask it.

SKIM ALL THE QUESTIONS

Before writing, skim all the questions so you can plan on how much time to spend on each. Keep to your plan. Remember, an unanswered question is a guaranteed zero.

THE EASIEST ONE FIRST

Do the easy ones to begin with. Most athletes are no strangers to the notion of momentum. Answering the easy questions gets you started right away, so by the time you reach the hard ones, you're on a winning streak.

THE CARDINAL RULE

Don't get stuck on any one question. Don't freeze. Skip it and get going. Time's precious. One more thing—when you come across a question that stumps you, don't get upset. Don't run the clock down by pondering or worrying. Go on to the next. Keep your balance, confidence, and dignity.

EARLY FINISH

Don't leave the room until they throw you out. Go over everything. Add a line here or there on an essay answer. Correct spelling. Put in punctuation. Many games are won by stick-to-it-tiveness.

AFTER THE EXAM

TALK IT OVER

While your memory is still fresh, talk over the exam with several of your friends. You'll hear the techniques and reasoning procedures that other students used to tackle the same problems that you faced. Information of this sort can help you to do a better job on the next exam.

FIVE WAYS TO PUT A GRADED EXAM TO GOOD USE

1. Look over the question you missed and try to find out where and why you went wrong.

2. Outline or write out better answers for the questions you missed as though you were given a second chance. You may actually get a second chance. Instructors frequently include a question or two from a previous test in the next exam.

3. Find out why your right answers are correct. You'll be amazed how much you'll learn about answering questions correctly.

4. Figure out which questions or types of questions gave you the most trouble. Pinpoint, if you can, the source of the troublesome questions. Did they come from lectures, texts, or discussions? You should learn where to put the extra emphasis in the future.

5. Decide which of your test-taking strategies worked and which did not. Make changes *now* before you risk making the same mistakes twice.

INSTRUCTOR

I think that it is a great idea to meet with the instructor, not to argue, but to seek suggestions that will help you on your next exam. Before the meeting, write out the questions you want to ask. Make sure that they are phrased in a constructive manner. Be sure to ask the instructor how you should have answered some specific questions; or, how you could have improved a fairly good answer. I guarantee that you'll learn more from such a constructive meeting than you thought possible. Furthermore, nothing will warm an instructor's heart more than meeting with a student who is trying to learn, trying to improve.

Needless to say, above all, do not argue or complain about any of the questions or any of the grading. Make this a positive meeting.

A Few Tips

1. Throughout the semester, strive mighty hard to complete term and research papers when they are first assigned; otherwise, they will not only haunt you, but also, destroy your plans for studying for and taking exams.

2. Don't skip classes at any time; especially around exam time. Instructors often sum up their courses near the end, and also give hints about the exam. These are too good to miss.

3. During exam-studying week, make up a new time schedule to include your regular responsibilities, plus definite times to study definite subjects for the up-coming exams.

4. Make up another special schedule for the week or period when you will be taking exams. Your time is very precious during this period; so, put your plan on paper and follow the plan.

Work Smarter, Not Harder

Five rules for success:
1. Always study the most important subject first.
2. Make friends with several of the smartest students in each of your classes; so, when you're absent because of travel, practice, or injury, you'll have notes to borrow and friends to tell what went on in class.
3. Get a high grade on the *first* exam by studying right from the first day of class. This high grade will help to carry you through the balance of the semester when practicing and playing consume a lot of your time.
4. Be a miser with daytime minutes. Don't leave much for the evening. Go to bed early and get up early. An hour's work in the morning is the way to start the day.
5. Take control of your life by making yourself do things when they are supposed to be done whether you like it or not.

Jay Gallagher, former *Assistant Coach, Cornell Lacrosse*

Vocabulary: Building a Background

> Definition: ath-lete—A person possessing the natural or acquired traits, such as strength, agility, and endurance, that are necessary for physical exercise or sports, especially those performed in competitive contexts.
>
> WORD HISTORY: *athlete*—one who contends for a prize. The ancestor of our modern *athlete* was the ancient Greek or Roman who entered the public games as a prize fighter or a contestant for a prize. The word *athlete* is borrowed from Latin *athleta* and that, in turn, from Greek *athletes*, "prize fighter." This word formed from *athlein*, "to contend for a prize," from *athlos*, "a contest," and *athlon*, " prize."

Words in Context

Directions: Make a light check mark (✓) alongside one of the two words (choices) that most nearly expresses the meaning of the italicized word in the episodes. (Answers are given on p. 126.) Excerpts reprinted courtesy of *SPORTS ILLUSTRATED*. Copyright ©, Time Inc. All rights reserved.

"I know Pat Tillman, Arizona State's linebacker, is ready to play in the NFL," says Von der Ahe. "He can play strong safety linebacker in a nickel package, somewhere. He's *tenacious*, he's smart, he's got great *instincts*."

| 67. he's *tenacious* | flexible | sticks to it |
| 68. great *instincts* | judgment | natural sense |

The Washington State Cougars are the Pac-10 co-champs, on their way to the Rose Bowl, but when they walk past a mirror, they see a *motley* band of *renegades* and rejects, *spurned* by other schools and *scoffed* at by national media. Many of them say they chose to attend Washington State for a simple reason: No one else wanted them.

69. a *motley* band	varied	identical
70. band of *renegades*	followers	rebels
71. *spurned* by others	rejected	inspired
72. *scoffed* at by	cheered	laughed at

Mike Keenan, the new coach of the Vancouver Canucks, has a program which *encompasses* everything from *refurbishing* the locker room to demanding superb conditioning, to *instituting* an up-tempo pressure game based on pursuit of the puck.

73. *encompasses* everything	ignores	includes
74. *refurbishing* the locker room	renovating	releasing
75. *instituting* an up-tempo	concluding	establishing

11
OBJECTIVE TESTS

Four types of test-questions are covered in this chapter (true-false, multiple-choice, matching, and sentence completion). To keep the many ideas in this chapter short and clear, we used the question-and-answer format. So, to get the most out of this chapter, we suggest you read the question first, imagining that you asked the question. Then, move to the right and read the answer, imagining that you are hearing the answer.

TRUE-FALSE QUESTIONS

QUALIFIERS

What makes true-false questions so difficult?   Qualifiers.

What are qualifiers?   They're like words like *some*, *most*, *all*, *often* and *usually*. Without them, true-false questions would be a breeze.

Take a look at the following examples:

Three True Statements

1. Dinosaurs are extinct.
2. Baseball stadiums have artificial turf.
3. Vice Presidents are elected.

Because they aren't specific, all of these statements are true. But when you add a qualifier to each statement, the picture changes somewhat.

One True Statement

1. *Most* dinosaurs are extinct.
2. *Some* baseball stadiums have artificial turf.
3. *All* Vice Presidents are elected.

Suddenly, the addition of qualifiers has left only one of the statements true.

Which One?

Let's go through them, one at a time.

1.   Most dinosaurs are extinct. Although there are some probable descendants of dinosaurs still walking the Earth today (many reptiles, for example) there is no creature alive that could be considered a dinosaur. Therefore, the statement "Most dinosaurs are extinct" is false. *All* dinosaurs are extinct.

*But doesn't **most** come close enough?*

Close only counts in horseshoes. Many of the true-false statements that you come across will be at least partially true. But only the statements that are *totally* true can be marked as true.

How about the next statement?

2.   Some baseball stadiums have artificial turf. Assume first that the question is referring to major league baseball stadiums. (If there is any doubt about a point like this, be sure to ask the instructor for clarification.) There are thirty stadiums in the major leagues. Only eleven of them have artificial turf. Therefore, it would be false to say that *most* of the stadiums have artificial turf because the total is less than half. However, the word *some*, although it isn't an accurate measurement, could be considered to make the sentence true.

Why is the last statement false?

3. All Vice Presidents are elected. Although the Constitution indicates that under normal circumstances the Vice President is elected, there have been two exceptions over the years. In 1973, after Vice President Spiro Agnew resigned, Gerald R. Ford became Vice President under Richard M. Nixon, without ever being elected. Less than a year later, when President Nixon resigned and Ford became President, Nelson A. Rockefeller became the second non-elected Vice President out of a total of 47 Vice Presidents in American history. Therefore, it cannot be correct to say that *all* Vice Presidents are elected.

*Are **all**, **most** and **some** the only qualifiers?*

No, there are quite a few more. In fact, there are 19 common qualifiers, which occur in six basic sets. It would be a good idea to memorize them.

Six Sets of Common Qualifiers

1. All, most, some, none (no)
2. Always, usually, sometimes, never
3. Great, much, little, no
4. More, equal, less
5. Good, bad
6. Is (are), is not (are not)

What good does it do to learn these qualifiers by heart?

Once you know the qualifiers and the set from which they originate, you're well on your way to tackling an otherwise difficult true-false question.

How do I do that?

By replacing the qualifier in the sentence with the other qualifiers of the set until you come up with a sentence that is true.

Using Qualifiers to Solve a True-False Question

1. Find the qualifier in the true-false statement.
2. Decide which set the qualifier belongs to.
3. Mentally replace the qualifier with each member of the qualifier set.
4. If none of the replacements seem to make the sentence true, then the statement was probably true in the first place.
5. If one of the qualifiers does seem to make the sentence true, then the original statement is probably false.

Is that all I need to know in order to solve true-false statements?	Unfortunately, no. There are some other elements of true-false statements that you should be on the lookout for.
Such as?	One hundred percent words. This is the name that I give to those qualifiers which say that a statement is true without exception.
For example?	The statement we just analyzed, about the Vice Presidents, is a perfect example. The qualifier *all* is a one hundred percent word. It says that there is no middle ground.
It's all or nothing?	Right! In fact, *all* and *nothing* are both one hundred percent words. Here is a list of the most common ones.

No	Every	Only
Never	Always	Entirely
None	All	Invariably
Nothing	Best	

What should I do if I find a statement which contains a one hundred percent word?	Be on your guard. There are very few statements in the world that are one hundred percent true. As a result, these qualifiers almost always signal a false statement.
Are these words ever a part of a true statement?	Yes, occasionally. Therefore, you shouldn't mark one of these statements false automatically. Here are some examples of one hundred percent statements that are true:

> *None of the jurors may disagree in order for a defendant to be proven guilty.*

> *All people need air in order to survive.*

> *Every National Football League player is paid to play.*

If there are exceptions, then what good is the rule?	The advantage of knowing about one-hundred percent words is that once you spot them, the statement should be presumed false instead of true. That way, if you can't find a reason that the statement is true, you can mark it false with confidence. Furthermore, if you are running out of time, the odds are with you if you quickly mark all the hundred percent statements false.
Are there any other types of qualifiers that I should be looking out for?	Yes, there's one more: the in-between words.

seldom	*many*	*ordinarily*
sometimes	*few*	*frequently*
often	*usually*	*some*
most	*generally*	

And what's the rule with in-between words?	Just the opposite of hundred percent words. Because these words fall in between the two extremes, they are generally true. Here are two examples, both true: *Ordinarily, the Vice President is elected.* *Basketball players are usually over six feet tall.*

Long Statements

Is there anything about the way that a true-false statement looks which may give me a clue as to whether it is true or false?	Yes, there is. Long statements will often be false.
Why is that?	I already mentioned that in order for a statement to be true, each part of the statement must be true. Long statements have more parts and, as a result, there is a greater chance that one of the parts will be false.

So should I mark all long statements false?

No, but you should view them suspiciously. Don't stop reading a lengthy statement as soon as you find out that part of it is true. The rest of it might be false. Here are two examples of false statements:

A physical education teacher named James Naismith organized the world's first basketball game in 1891 at a college gymnasium in Springfield, Illinois.

Aerobic exercises, which involve prolonged infusion of oxygen into the cardio-pulmonary system, include running, swimming, bike riding, and golf.

Both of these sentences may be marked "True" by the careless test taker, even if he or she happens to know the facts. Yet neither is completely true.

So, how do I prevent myself from incorrectly marking a false statement?

When you encounter a long statement you should use a kind of mental check list to verify the validity of each part of the statement.

For example?

_____ Naismith was a physical education teacher.
_____ Naismith's first name was James.
_____ Naismith organized the world's first basketball game.
_____ The game was played in 1891.
_____ It took place in a college gymnasium.
_____ The gym was located in the town of Springfield.
_____ The Springfield where the game occurred was in Illinois.

The last statement is false: Naismith invented basketball in Springfield, *Massachusetts.*

That's an awfully tricky question.	True. You may not run into a question like that all that often. Nevertheless, the principle is the same with simpler statements. A statement cannot be true unless each part of it is true. In the second example, there is only one word which makes this sentence false: golf. Because golf cannot be considered aerobic, the entire sentence is false.
Are there other variations of this partially true type of question?	There's a way that a statement can be made up of two true statements and still be false.
How can that be?	It happens when the two statements don't logically follow each other. The culprit is usually the conjunction, a word like *therefore*, *because,* or *consequently*.
For example?	The following two statements are true.

> *Elbert (Ickey) Woods rushed for 27 touchdowns in just 37 games.*
> *Following each touchdown, he did the Ickey Shuffle.*

But when you put them together they are false.

> *Because of the Ickey Shuffle, Elbert (Ickey) Woods scored 27 touchdowns.*

When the two statements are put together, they reach a conclusion that doesn't logically follow. And yet, if you read the statement quickly and didn't notice the key word, because, you would probably mark the answer "True."

Negatives

What else besides one hundred percent and conjunction qualifiers will change the meaning of a true-false statement?

Negatives, double negatives, and even triple negatives can make a simple sentence appear hopelessly difficult.

*Are you talking about words like **no** and **not**?*

Yes, but that's only part of it. There are quite a few negative prefixes that can reverse the meaning of a sentence. Although they have the same effect as no or not, these prefixes are often a little more difficult to pick out right away.

What happens if there is more than one negative?

Whether the sentence has one negative or ten, the procedure is the same.
1. Circle any and all negatives.
2. Try to get the meaning of the sentence without the negatives.
3. Add the negatives one by one and see how each changes the meaning of the sentence.

That seems like it could take a long time.

It could, especially if the sentence has a lot of negatives. If time is short and the negatives are plentiful, you might try this rule of thumb. It's about ninety percent accurate.
1. Circle any and all negatives.
2. Try to get the meaning of the sentence without the negatives. Is it true or false?
3. Count the number of negatives. If the number is *even*, then the meaning of the sentence should be the same as it was without the negatives. If the number of negatives is *odd*, the meaning should be the opposite of what it was without the negatives.

GUESSING THE ANSWERS TO TRUE-FALSE QUESTIONS

If I don't know the answer to a true-false question, is it worth a guess?

Definitely. But if you do guess, try to do so intelligently. Here are two guidelines for guessing:

1. **Most true-false tests contain more true statements than false ones**. That's because your instructor wants you to remember information that is accurate.

2. Guessing pays off even if points are taken off for each wrong answer. No test question has better odds. Each true-false question gives you a fifty-fifty chance to begin with. If you know something about the subject, your odds improve.

MULTIPLE CHOICE QUESTIONS

THE FUNDAMENTALS

Are all multiple choice questions written about the same way?

Basically. Although some feature complete sentences, most use an incomplete sentence known as a stem. The rest of the sentence lies below in one of the four or five options. The incorrect options are known as *decoys* or *distracters*.

And only the correct option will complete the sentence?

No. If the question is well-written, all of the options will complete the sentence. But only the correct option will complete it *correctly*.

What's the first step in answering a multiple choice question?

Read the directions. Although most multiple choice questions ask you to choose the single best answer, the directions will vary from time to time. You may be asked to circle the "two best answers," or "all correct answers" instead.

And after I've read the directions?

Start by reading the stem all the way through. (It's risky to read only part of it.) Then read every single option.

Do I need to read all the options if I've found the correct one?	Yes. You can't know for sure which option or options are correct until you have read every single one. In many cases, all of the options will make the sentence true but only one option will be the *best* option.
Is there any point in reading options if the question sounds unfamiliar?	Yes. Sometimes the options will let you know what the question is getting at, even if the stem has you confused. In other cases, a particular option may serve to trigger your memory.
What if I can't answer the question right away?	Skip it for the moment. You can come back later, if you have a chance. If you've done a little work on the question, be sure to mark the options that you were able to eliminate so you won't have to start from square one when you come back to it.
Should I handle the question any differently on the second time around?	Yes. This time, if you haven't already, try to make a definite effort to eliminate one or two options.
But isn't it tough to eliminate one or two options from a multiple choice question?	Not really. Often an option or two can be eliminated even if you don't know the material all that well. Of course, if you do know the material, your chances of weeding out the distracters are even greater. Here is the rule of thumb for guessing on multiple choice questions.

If 5 choices are given and you can
    eliminate 2 . . . *then guess.*

If 4 choices are given and you can
    eliminate 1 . . . *then guess.*

If you are unable to eliminate any
    choices . . . *skip the question.*

CLUES YOU CAN USE IF YOU DON'T KNOW YOUR MATERIAL

How can I get rid of options if I don't know the material?

There are six methods that you can use for narrowing your choices even if you don't know the material.
1. Watch out for 100% words.
2. Get rid of foolish options.
3. "All of the above" is usually correct.
4. The long answer is seldom wrong.
5. Check for look-alikes.
6. In number questions, pick a number in the middle range.

1. WATCH OUT FOR 100% WORDS.

Are the 100% words in a multiple choice question the same as those in a true-false?

Yes, they are. In fact, the same rules apply. You should be extremely suspicious of an option which contains a 100% word. Of course, as before, there are exceptions, so don't eliminate these options automatically unless you are pressed for time.

2. GET RID OF FOOLISH OPTIONS.

What do you mean by foolish options?

Although they may be humorous, foolish options are giveaways, pure and simple. They are usually included when the instructor can't come up with enough legitimate options. When you spot a foolish option, get rid of it right away.

3. "ALL OF THE ABOVE" IS USUALLY CORRECT.

Why is "All of the above" usually correct?

Remember that the main purpose of an objective test is to teach you facts. Therefore, if the instructor has an opportunity to squeeze in more than one act per question, he or she will probably do so. "All of the above" is an excellent way to accomplish this. Therefore, consider this option correct until you can prove it wrong.

4. The Long Answer is Seldom Wrong.

What does an answer's length have to do with whether it is correct or not?

It isn't as easy as you think to write a correct answer. It must be accurate and complete. Inexperienced testmakers will sometimes over amplify or over-qualify the correct option in order to insure that it is completely correct. If this happens, you're in luck. The correct answer will stand out like a basketball player at a hockey convention?

Do more experienced testmakers make the correct answer short?

Not necessarily. Experts on multiple choice test making know that the best procedure is to make all of the options roughly the same length.

5. Check for Look-alikes.

Are those the look-alikes that you refer to in the fifth rule?

No. Look-alikes are options that differ by only a word or two.

Can you give me an example?

Sure.
Dave DeBusschere
a. hit "The shot heard round the world" in the 1951 World Series.
b. played both professional basketball and professional baseball.
c. won the Davis Cup in 1968, 1971, and 1974.
d. played both professional soccer and professional basketball.

So options b and d are the look-alikes?

Right. And option b is the correct answer. DeBusschere played baseball briefly for the Chicago White Sox. Of course, he is better known as a basketball Hall-of-Famer who once played for the New York Knicks.

So should I always pick a look-alike option if I have the choice?

Not always. But if you're in a situation where you have to guess, I'd say it's a fairly good bet.

6. Pick a Number in the Middle Range.

What does the last rule refer to?

Some questions, particularly those in the sciences, have numbers for answers. It has been discovered, that for some reason, testmakers have a tendency to bracket number answers with a distracter that is higher and one that is lower than the correct answer. If you have to guess, get rid of these two numbers and pick your answer from the options that remain.

Clues You Can Use If You Know Your Material

*Are there some special methods that you can use if you **do** know your material?*

Yes, in fact, there are three of them.
1. Use the true-false technique.
2. Stick to the subject matter.
3. Watch out for negatives.

Use the True-False Technique.

Many students prefer true-false to multiple choice because they feel that answering a true-false question is easier. If you're one of those people, you might try using the true-false technique.

And what is the true-false technique?

Almost any multiple choice question can be seen as a series of true-false statements. Each statement begins with the stem and ends with an option. To use the true-false technique simply reconnect the stem to the option and decide whether the statement that results is true or false. If it's false, the option is a distracter. If it's true, then you have spotted the correct option.

Is this method of any use if you don't have trouble with multiple choice questions?

Yes. The true-false technique can also serve as a way of checking your answer even if you have no trouble with the multiple choice format.

STICK TO THE SUBJECT MATTER.

Don't all multiple choice questions stick to the subject matter?

They're supposed to but that isn't always the case. One of the best ways to strike fear into the heart of the test taking student is to include a choice that is unfamiliar.

But isn't it easy to tell that the option doesn't belong?

You'd be surprised. When nerves are on edge and confidence is low, otherwise intelligent students will select options that have nothing to do with the subject matter, going on the false assumption that an option wouldn't be included if it didn't have something to do with the question. Well, the fact is that irrelevant options are included from time to time, and like the foolish options that we have already discussed, they can be eliminated right away.

WATCH OUT FOR NEGATIVES.

Do you treat negatives the same way with multiple choice questions as you do with true-false statements?

Pretty nearly. The one variation that you may find with negatives in a multiple choice question is that they can be in the stem as well as in the options. If you have any doubt as to their effect on the meaning of the question, my advice is to use the true-false technique and then handle the negatives as we did with true-false statements.

MATCHING QUESTIONS

THE FUNDAMENTALS

In what type of class am I likely to run into a matching test?

Matching tests are popular in almost any course where definitions, dates or terms need to be remembered.

What does the standard matching test look like?	Normally it will have two vertical lines of items placed side by side. Both lists will be in random order. Often, but not always, the items on one list will be more brief than those on the other. The task is to connect an item from one list to an item from the other. The directions will tell you what sort of relationship should exist between the two.
Is there some secret to answering matching questions?	Not exactly. The best way to excel on any test is to master the material you need to know. However, you can learn to answer a matching test as efficiently and effectively as possible.
What's the first thing I should do to answer a matching question?	Step one is the same for every type of test questions: read the directions. Make sure you know what's involved before you begin. Glance down the columns of items so you are familiar with what you'll be matching.
Should I match the items in any order?	Yes. It is a good idea to begin by reading the item at the top of the left-hand column. Then go down the right-hand column and see if you can find a match.
When I find a match, should I go on to the next items in the left-hand column?	Don't be so hasty! If you think you've found a match for the first item, don't stop yet. Keep looking down the column to make sure there isn't a better match. Check every choice before you make a connection.
What if I'm not sure that the match is a good one?	If you have the slightest doubt, don't mark anything. If you do mark and the answer turns out to be wrong, you could get yourself hopelessly confused.
What should I do instead?	Now is the time to go on to the next item in the left-hand column.

Should I leave that one blank if I can't find a certain match?	Yes, you should. The trick to answering a matching test is to mark only the matches that you know for sure. This is like narrowing your options in a multiple choice test. Once you have the sure things marked you can go back to the items you left blank. With less of a selection you should have an easier job making the matches that remain.
Are there any other hints that will help me to answer a matching test?	One more: it is a good idea to circle the letter or number alongside each match as soon as you've used it. This will give you a clearer idea of what choices remain.

STUDYING FOR MATCHING TESTS

Now that you've explained how to answer matching tests, is there anything I can do that will help me to study for them?	Yes, there is. It helps, first, to know if your instructor is liable to include matching questions on the exam. If you're expecting a matching test, you can start to be alert for definitions and terms at the very beginning of the semester.
Is simply being aware of the fact that I may have a matching test going to do me any good?	Being in the proper mindset for a matching test can help quite a bit. However, you can take your studying a step further. Throughout the semester you can keep a running list of all the terms and definitions that might appear on a matching test.
Should I prepare my own practice matching test?	No, at least not right away. The better idea is to arrange the information in proper order instead of in the random order that it will appear on your test. Then cover up one column with a blank piece of paper. Take each item in the exposed column one at a time and recite, aloud and from memory, the item that matches with it.

That sounds a lot like reciting notes with the Cornell System.

That's no coincidence. A matching test is like two cue columns. Once you've gone through the list several times, reverse the process by uncovering the other column and reciting the column you've just read, from memory. Then, once you feel as though you've mastered the material, you might try scrambling the items and then matching them up.

SENTENCE-COMPLETION QUESTIONS

I have a rough time with sentence completion questions because there are no answers from which to choose.

Believe it or not, these questions are tougher on the test maker than they are on the test taker. After all, you only have to fill in the blank. The person who makes up the test has to write the question in such a way that there's only one correct answer.

So why don't instructors stick to multiple choice, true-false, and matching questions? I wouldn't mind.

I'm sure you wouldn't. But sentence-completion questions serve a purpose. They're designed to build up your recall just as other questions strengthen your recognition.

What is recognition?

Recognition is the skill you need when you answer true-false, multiple choice, and matching questions. In each case, all you need to do is to recognize the correct answer.

And recall?

That's what sentence-completion questions require. The emphasis is put on your memory. You actually have to recall the correct answer. It's not a matter of pick and choose.

Doesn't that make sentence-completion questions a lot more difficult?

Not really. You have to know your material for every type of question. The only difference is that you aren't able to guess as successfully.

How are most sentence-completion questions set up?	The standard sentence-completion question has only one blank. Normally you are expected to fill in the blank with only one word, not an insurmountable task, providing that the question has been written properly and you have done your homework. Of course, your job gets even easier if the blank is at the end of the sentence.
Why's that?	With the blank at the end, you have uninterrupted context of the sentence to help you to complete your answer.
Are two blanks harder?	Not harder really, just different. There are two variations of the two-blank sentence-completion question. The blanks may be consecutive or they may be widely separated.
How do you handle a two-blank sentence when the blanks are consecutive?	This type of question usually calls for a name. Although it may not be as simple as the single blank at the end of the sentence, it is a great help to know what kind of answer you are looking for. That really narrows things down.
Doesn't the length of the blanks make things even easier?	No. It is usually a big mistake to pick your answer based on the length of the blanks. A short blank won't always mean a short name. Whether the answer is Babe Ruth or Abner Doubleday, the blanks should be the same size.
What happens when the blanks are separated?	Obviously the situation is quite different. Simply because the two blanks occur in the same sentence leaves no guarantee that the missing words will be related. The best idea is to treat each blank as though it appears in a separate sentence.

Don't some sentences have extra long blanks?

Yes, if there is only one blank and it is especially long, it is safe to assume that the test maker is looking for a phrase or clause.

Guessing won't help in this kind of question, will it?

Put it this way: if you don't know the answer already, there's little chance that you will come up with it by accident. However, that doesn't mean that you shouldn't take a stab at it. Even if your response doesn't mesh with the instructor's, you may get partial credit for coming close.

I would think that the long blank questions would start a lot of arguments.

They do. That's the main reason that many instructors stay away from them.

Now that I know the forms that a sentence-completion question can take, are there any clues that will help me to get the answer?

Naturally, because your choices aren't written out, there are no clues that will point to a specific answer. However, you can use grammar as well as some carefully phrased questions to narrow your choices quite a bit.

How is grammar going to help me to fill in the blank properly?

Because your blank occurs in a sentence, it must adhere to the rules of grammar, just as any other word in the sentence.

For example? This one is a giveaway.
1. *According to recent NCAA statistics, about _____ in six college soccer players is a woman.*

You don't have to know a thing about soccer or the latest statistics in order to answer this question. However, you do need to understand sentence construction. Because the word *woman* is singular, it follows that the word in the blank must be singular as well. The only number which fits that description is *one*.

Are there any other grammatical clues which will aid me in answering a sentence-completion question?

Yes, there is one more. I call it the *a or an clue*. *A* is that article used before nouns that begin with consonants, as in

a *player*	a *field goal*	a *penalty*
a *catcher*	a *serve*	a *referee*

while *an* is used before nouns that begin with vowels, as in

an *athlete*	an *extra point*	an *infraction*
an *outfielder*	an *ace*	an *umpire*

Knowing this simple fact can help you to narrow your choices considerably whenever you encounter a blank that is preceded by an *a* or *an*.

Are many questions set up that way?

Unfortunately, they're not as common as they used to be. Many instructors realize that their students are wise to this clue and so they make an effort to avoid the situation altogether. Others get around it by using the frustrating "a(n)" in place of both *a* and *an*.

What is the question asking strategy?

All it really means is that if you come across a question that needs clarification, by all means, don't be afraid to ask.

What should I ask?

That all depends on the test question. Whatever you ask, make sure your question is well-formulated and precise. Unless you ask exactly what you need to know, you run the risk of getting a vague response to your vague question. Or, as the saying goes, ask a silly question, get a silly answer.

For example?

Suppose the question said:
> *In the whole of last season, _____ led the NBA in scoring.*

If you asked, "Are you looking for a singular answer or a plural answer?" you wouldn't get any response that would be helpful in answering the question.

But, if you asked, "Are you looking for a player or a team?" you would receive the clarification you needed.

Asking a question is a little like writing a sentence-completion question. If you are to be successful, you must be absolutely sure that your question can be interpreted in only one way.

Is there any point in guessing on a sentence-completion question?

Although I already mentioned that guessing was difficult with a sentence-completion question, this does not mean that you should leave any of the blanks without answers. Guessing on a question is always better than taking a sure zero.

Is there a special procedure for guessing on a sentence-completion question?

Not really. It's about the same as with most questions. Here is a procedure for guessing on sentence-completion questions.
1. Go through the entire test first, answering only the questions you are sure of.
2. Mark the questions that you are unable to answer.
3. On the second pass, read each unanswered question over again.
4. If you are still unable to answer it, make a guess, based on common sense, as to what you think the answer should be.

Vocabulary: Building a Background

Definition: gym-na-si-um—Sports. A room or building equipped for indoor sports.

WORD HISTORY: *gymnasium*—no longer in its literal meaning. In the golden age of Athens, athletics played an important part in Greek life, and physical strength and grace were highly regarded. The athletes, in their games, were not impeded by costumes; they exercised nude. "Nude" in Greek is *gymnos*. The derivative *gymnazein* means "to exercise (nude)." A *gymnasion* was a "place where athletic exercises were performed (in the nude)." This is the source of our own word *gymnasium*, which has retained the sense of activity if not that of costume.

Words in Context

Directions: Make a light check mark (✓) alongside one of the two words (choices) that most nearly expresses the meaning of the italicized word in the episodes. (Answers are given on p. 126.) Excerpts reprinted courtesy of *SPORTS ILLUSTRATED*. Copyright ©, Time Inc. All rights reserved.

To get and keep himself in tip-top shape, Jerry Rice, the great pass receiver of the San Francisco 49ers, goes for a *brisk* run up the *infamous* Portola Valley hill that has been a *staple* of his off-season training *regimen* throughout the 90s. Says one veteran, "Jerry should wait until he's right and wait until next year." The veteran continues, "You can see that he's pressing, and he's putting his career in *jeopardy*. Any defensive back he faces is going to try to take him out."

76. a *brisk* run	tiring	quick
77. *infamous* Portola Valley hill	detestable	splendid
78. has been a *staple*	distraction	feature
79. his training *regimen*	program	recommendation
80. career in *jeopardy*	security	danger

Just as veteran Freddie Solomon helped Jerry Rice in his *rookie* season, Rice has no *qualms* about *tutoring* J.J. Stokes and Terrell Owens, who are aiming to displace him. "Hey, I could stick around as the third receiver," Jerry says. "That might *prolong* my career another 10 years."

81. his *rookie* season	middle	beginning
82. has no *qualms*	plans	uneasiness
83. about *tutoring*	teaching	criticizing
84. *prolong* my career	limit	extend

12
TAKING ESSAY TESTS

Essay questions are great because they give you a chance to do it "your way." You have a chance to express what you learned and what you know. Multiple choice and true-false questions have their place, but there you just encircle this or that. The essay permits creativity, to "tailor make" your answer.

SHORT-ANSWER QUESTIONS

Short-answer questions are really mini-essay questions. These questions require an ability to interpret the directions and express answers clearly and completely, all in a limited amount of time. Here are four tips that should help you answer short-answer questions more successfully.

1. THINK BEFORE YOU WRITE. This way you can be sure you're using words efficiently and effectively.
2. GIVE DIRECT ANSWERS. Your main goal is to present information.
3. USE TELEGRAPHIC SENTENCES. It's the facts, not the frills that count. If your instructor requires complete sentences, make them short and to the point.
4. WORK THROUGH THE TEST TWICE. On the first pass, answer only the questions you are sure of. Mark the questions you have skipped. On your second trip, re-think the troublesome questions and write down any fragments you can recall. If these bits and pieces are put in a logical order, you are more likely to receive credit.

ESSAY QUESTIONS

The four tips stated previously for short-answer questions apply to long essay questions too. The only major difference is that your sentences must be complete, not telegraphic.

Taking the Exam

PREPARATION
Of course, you must know your material; but during the process of learning, think about these three questions and come up with definite answers.
1. *What type of question is the instructor most likely to ask?*
2. *What type of question has caused me the most trouble in the past?*
3. *What kind of question do **I want** to answer?*

FIRST STEP
Immediately turn the sheet over and on the backside quickly write a few facts, dates, or figures that you had memorized before forgetting occurs. This writing now frees your mind to concentrate on the questions.

READ THE DIRECTIONS AND QUESTIONS
While reading the directions, circle the key words. Often, you'll be given a choice—"answer three out of the five questions." So, read all the questions and pick out the ones you want to answer. As you read, circle the key words in the questions, too.

JOTTING IN THE MARGIN
As you read each question, jot cue words and phrases in the margin alongside the questions to which they refer.

MAKE A TIME PLAN
Before beginning to write, notice the amount of time left. Divide the time by the number of questions, giving yourself at least five minutes leeway at the end to look over your answers. Once made, stick to your time plan.

Easiest Questions First

Build momentum and confidence by answering the easiest questions first. Remember to number your answers.

Special Terms

In reading the questions, you should always circle any of the key terms listed in Figure 12.1. It is vitally important that you know what these specific terms require you to do. If in doubt, raise your hand and, in a well-phrased question, ask the person in charge.

Figure 12.1 Special Terms

Key Words in Essay Questions

Apply principle–Show how principle works through an example.

Comment–Discuss briefly.

Compare–Emphasize similarities but also differences.

Contrast–Give only the differences.

Criticize–Give your judgments, as to good points, drawbacks.

Define–Supply meanings without details.

Demonstrate–Show or prove your opinion, evaluation, or judgment.

Describe–State in detail the particulars.

Diagram–Show drawing with labels.

Differentiate–Show how two things are different.

Discuss–Give reasons, pro and con, with details.

Distinguish–Show main point between two things, how different.

Enumerate–List the points.

Evaluate–Discuss advantages and disadvantages; your opinion, too.

Identify–Describe events, places, or persons.

Illustrate–Give an example.

Interpret–Give your judgment.

Justify–Prove or give reasons.

List–List without details.

Outline–Make a short summary of heads and subheads.

Prove–Give evidence and reasons.

Purpose–Tell how something fulfills the overall design.

Relate–Show how things interconnect.

Review–Show main points or events in summary form.

Show–List your evidence in order of time, importance, logic.

State–List main points briefly, without details.

Solve–Come up with your solution from given facts.

Summarize–Organize and bring together main points only.

Support–Back up your statements with facts and proof.

Trace–Give main points from beginning to end of an event.

Outline Your Answer

How? Remember those jottings of cue words and phrases in the margins? Well, number them in the order that you plan to write your answer. This numbering will put your points in some organized structure, and with almost no waste of time.

Organization Principle

The best principle for organization is *one idea–one paragraph*. If you hop back and forth from one idea to another, the focus of your answer may be blurred.

Writing the Answer: The Introduction

No introduction. Why? An introduction forces you to scatter your ideas. It causes you to damage the unity of your answer; consequently, the focus is bound to be blurred.

Opening Sentence

The first sentence is all-important; probably, the most important in the whole essay. A sure way to come up with a winner is this: start your sentence by repeating the question and carrying it on to your direct answer. For example, if the question were, "How do you come up with a strong focus in an essay answer?" you would answer, "You come up with a strong focus by answering the question in the very first sentence."

Notice the direct, simple, strong answer. There's no introduction to blur; no beating around the bush. The answer, like an arrow, heads straight for the bull's eye.

Another Example

Question: The price of gold shot up. Why?
Answer: The price of gold shot up for the following four reasons.
Comment: Notice how clean, crisp, and easy it is to start off with the words in the question itself. This way puts and keeps you on the right track.

Rest of the Essay

The rest of the essay provides the facts, ideas, and details that will support your answer, which is the first sentence. In writing, use signal words (*first, second, finally, more important*), as well as transitional words (*in summary, on the one hand, in contrast, in conclusion*) to let the reader know what you are saying and why.

Long Essays

If your essay is ten or fifteen minutes long, you should put your answer in the first paragraph. Use, of course, the same approach of repeating the question in the first sentence of your first paragraph. Then, the paragraphs that follow will act as supporting material for your first paragraph.

Best for Last?

No, never! That's a risky idea. If your answer doesn't come in the first few lines, the instructor might not be clear on the point that you are making. Furthermore, if you delay your answer too long, you may find that you aren't even able to work it into your essay at all; at least, logically.

Ending Your Essay

You should use the last few sentences of your essay to summarize or repeat the point that you made in your first sentence or paragraph. In other words, in your last sentence or paragraph, you need to "round" off your essay.

Tips for Taking Essay Tests

1. Stick to the facts. As Hugo Hartig, a professor of English, puts it . . . "it is important to remember that liking or disliking is irrelevant; understanding is all important."
2. Write carefully. Pages and pages of sloppy writing will not earn points for you; but, a neatly written answer will often earn more points than you may truly deserve.
3. No snow jobs. Phony answers will stick out like a sore thumb to the trained eye of the professor.
4. Complex ideas. Some of the world's more complex ideas can be expressed in straightforward and simple language. Make simplifying the complex one of your prime goals.
5. Use ink. Pencil is not appropriate for an essay exam.
6. Use only one side of each sheet. This will prevent the previous page from showing through. It will also give you room for insertions, if you need them.
7. Leave a generous left-hand margin. Your paper will look neater and the grader will have room for comments.
8. Leave spaces between your answers. This will provide room in case you want to add to your answer later.

9. WATCH THE TIME. If it runs out unexpectedly, outline the points that you were planning to make. You will very likely get some credit. If you have extra time, go back and check over your answers.

10. NOT ANSWERING IS A GUARANTEED ZERO. If you have time left, never leave an essay question unanswered. Write something; but, of course, don't write trash. Do this: think calmly for a minute. Jot down a cue word or phrase of anything related to the topic that pops into your head. Quickly number them for organization; then, write neatly, correctly, and vigorously. As you write and think, you might dredge up some hidden thought. So, on a 10-point question, you might get 2, 3, or 4. Well, this is better than zero; but, it's no gift. You earned it!

VOCABULARY: BUILDING A BACKGROUND

Definition: pen-cil—A narrow, generally cylindrical implement for writing, consisting of a thin rod of graphite encased in wood or held in a mechanical holder.

> WORD HISTORY: *pencil*—from a little tail. The Latin *penicillus*, meaning "a little tail," is the ancestor of our word *pencil*. The term *pencil* was first applied to a brush of hair or bristles used by artists and suggestive, in its form, of the "little tail" from which it was named. Later, the word took on its present common meaning.

WORDS IN CONTEXT

Directions: Make a light check mark (✓) alongside one of the two words (choices) that most nearly expresses the meaning of the italicized word in the episodes. (Answers are given on p. 126.) Excerpts reprinted courtesy of *SPORTS ILLUSTRATED*. Copyright ©, Time Inc. All rights reserved.

The 7'11", 315 pound Shaquille O'Neal of the Los Angeles Lakers somehow *maneuvered* his *gargantuan* body through a *maze* of defenders and scored on a nifty little layup, which he *punctuated* with an *imitation* of San Francisco 49er Merton Hands's *spasmodic* "chicken dance," although it looked like a loss of all motor control.

85. *maneuvered* his body	plowed	steered
86. his *gargantuan* body	athletic	enormous
87. through a *maze*	mass	pattern
88. which he *punctuated*	emphasized	underplayed
89. with an *imitation*	copy	celebration
90. *spasmodic* dance	smooth	jerky

Several veteran players likewise overcame their *allegiance* to a teammate, Latrell Sprewell. "You can't *condone* it," says Bogues, saying they supported the player, but not the play, and asked the rest of the team to come together and produce something more presentable than outright *disintegration*.

91. their *allegiance*	loyalty	coolness
92. can't *condone* it	pardon	condemn
93. outright *disintegration*	coming together	falling apart

"Baron Davis has a real *passion* for the game that you can see on both ends of the court," says UCLA coach Steve Lavin. "His *insatiable* desire to learn is what really separates him from other players his age."

94. real *passion*	spirit	talent
95. his *insatiable*	bottomless	natural

> *Don't Let Time Run Out on You*
> If a student uses bits and pieces of time throughout the day, plus a couple of solid hours in the early evening, there'll be enough time for athletics, academics, social living, and sleep; but, mind you, the student must be in complete command of time.
>
> ANDY NOEL, former *Head Coach, Cornell Wrestling*

13
WRITING THE
RESEARCH PAPER

Here's what I'd do if I were a student again. The very day that the assignment is given, I'd take immediate action by going to the library to seek a topic that would not only fit the assignment perfectly, but also fit my own personal interests. Then, I'd follow the step-by-step research process put forth in this chapter.

What usually makes a research paper a horror? It's when students begin a frantic search for material only a few days before the paper is due. Then, the paper is thrown together, and it looks it. Of course, with luck, it'll receive a low C or a high D.

But stop to look at what could be: by starting on the very first day, and bit by bit, the paper should bring you not only real satisfaction, but also, a fairly sure A.

CHOOSING A TOPIC

This is the most crucial part of writing a research paper. Choosing a workable topic is a three step process.

Step 1:   Choose a topic that interests you.
Step 2:   Narrow your topic.
Step 3:   Provide a focus.

THE ASSIGNMENT

Let's start with the instructor. He/She usually picks the *subject*, but, in almost all cases, you pick the *topic*. Say the course is in twentieth century history, or economics, or labor relations, and the class is assigned, for example, to write about labor unions.

STEP 1: CHOOSE A TOPIC THAT INTERESTS YOU

Referring to the assignment, your first reaction might be, "Oh, no! I'm not interested in labor unions." "But wait," you say to yourself, "I can still pick a topic within the subject area."

Your main hope is to find a topic in the *Readers' Guide to Periodical Literature* or a computerized periodical listing. This *Guide* is found in the reference room of almost every library. These year by year volumes contain the titles and subject matter for most of the articles that have appeared in major magazines since World War I. So, you'll find current, up-to-date topics, as well as older topics, all written in popular style, making reading enjoyable and understanding easy.

So, under the alphabetical listings, you turn to "Labor Unions" and go down the columns, and as you turn the pages, you become discouraged. But, on the middle of the last page your eyes light up. You see, "Major League Baseball Strike." Now, you feel happy because you've found an interesting topic within a previously uninteresting subject area.

STEP 2: NARROW YOUR TOPIC

The rule to remember is that your title is a promise or a contract that you will cover whatever your title says it will. For example, if your full title is the "Major League Baseball Strike," then, you'll have to cover the topic from all sides: the players', the managements', and the public's. You'll need to write, at least, several books. So, to avoid promising too much, simply narrow your title in this way.

General Topic: 20th Century Labor Unions

1st narrowing: The 1985 strike involving the Major League Baseball Player's Association. (MLBPA)

2nd narrowing: How the 1985 baseball strike affected the labor-management relations.

3rd narrowing: How the 1985 baseball strike affected the players and the public.

4th narrowing: How the 1985 baseball strike affected the public.

Notice that each topic covers a narrower and narrower range. The point is this: cut the topic down to the size that you want to handle in depth.

Preliminary Research

Once you've narrowed your topic, see if you can find enough references to cover your topic. The best place to start is the *Reader's Guide to Periodical Literature*. Look under "Labor Unions," "Baseball," "Strikes," and "Major League Baseball Player's Association." If you find enough references, fine. But, if you don't, then switch your topic, or make it broader; but, don't try to squeeze water from a stone. In this case, however, I'm sure you'll find enough references. So, your next step is to provide a focus.

STEP 3: PROVIDE A FOCUS

You may have selected the world's most interesting topic, but without a focus it's little more than a collection of facts. All papers should pose one important question. That question will give your paper the direction and purpose it needs to hold itself together.

By taking your 4th narrowing and forming it into a question, you'll have a focus. The question now is: How did the 1985 baseball strike affect the public?

Having done this, all the information you gather should be to answer this one question. Even though you may find other fascinating facts, if they do not pertain to the question, leave them out.

For a full-fledge research paper, you are going to have to spend some time in the library. There are three areas in the library that should be helpful.

THE REFERENCE SECTION: Contains everything from phone books to encyclopedias. It is also the spot where you will find the current indexes for articles in magazines and journals. *The Reader's Guide* is located here. So is the *New York Times Index*, *The Business Periodicals Index*, and the *Education Index*, to name just a few.

THE PERIODICAL SECTION: As the name implies, this area houses most of the library's newspapers and magazines. After you've collected the titles of possible sources from the reference section, the periodical section is the place to go.

THE CARD CATALOG OR COMPUTERIZED INDEX: If your topic is a popular one, there will probably be some books written about it. The card catalog or computerized index lists the library's books, alphabetically, by author, by subject, and often, by title. Be sure to check several headings as you are searching for books. Some subjects may not have earned their own book, but may appear in other books.

RESEARCH CARDS

NOTE CARDS OR SLIPS

Now that you know where to go, here's how to take notes. Keep two sets of note cards: one set for bibliography and the other for the detailed notes you take from each article and book.

THE BIBLIOGRAPHY SET

Your bibliography set will be comprised of all the books, journals, magazines, and newspapers you plan to consult. Write each *complete* reference on a *separate* file card. Following is the format to use.

Format of the Bibliography Card

The front of the card

Library Name	Brief Title of Your Subject
Library Call number	Reference information in proper bibliographical form

Back of Bibliography Card

You'll want to skim and look over every reference. If it looks promising, write the comment on the back saying why. If the reference is a dud, say so. After looking over the dozens of books and magazine articles, the references tend to blur. Your notes will remind you of your original thoughts.

Notecards for Facts and Details

Ironclad rule: Each card should contain only one note; that is, only one piece of information, so when it comes time to write your paper, you can arrange each notecard in the order you want to use. If several notes were on one sheet of paper, you would be skipping back and forth, causing confusion and time-wasting.

Here are eleven tips for taking notes.

1. Use only one side of each slip for taking notes.
2. Identify the reference you used on each slip by writing the author's name or the book's title in the top left corner.
3. Write the page number where the note came from in the lower right.
4. Be sure to skim the article or chapter before you begin to take notes.
5. Write the notes in your own words. Not only will you understand them better, but, you will also get a head start on the actual writing of the paper.
6. Make your notes brief but detailed enough to provide accurate meaning.
7. Write neatly so you won't have to "translate" later.
8. Use ink. Notes taken in pencil are apt to blur with time.

9. Keep your direct quotations to a minimum. Most students tend to overdo it when it comes to quotations.
10. Abbreviate only the common words so you can be sure of what you've written later on.
11. If an idea occurs to you while you're taking notes, put it on a separate slip with the caption, "my own."

ORGANIZING YOUR PAPER

OUTLINE

You do not need a written outline. But, here's what to do to make an on-the-table outline. After you've taken all the notes you think you'll need, take the stack and deal them into topical piles on a big table; that is, cluster the notes bearing facts and details around major points.

ORGANIZING

Now that you have stacks of major points piled up, together with the minor points and details, it's time to shuffle these stacks into some order that makes sense to you. Just move the stacks around. After all, you've been reading and making notes for over several weeks; so, you have, by now, developed some feeling as to where the stacks belong.

QUESTIONS

You should, by now, be able to answer the following questions. Which side has the most evidence to support it? What should the basic theme or focus of my paper be? What do I want to say in my paper? Once you know the answers to these questions, you are ready to go back to your on-the-table outline and move the stacks around again until you have the major points in their proper order.

PRUNING

Now's the time to look at each stack and put to one side all the note slips that may be duplicates, as well as those slips you don't plan to use. Don't throw them away. Just take them out of the main stream.

BALANCE

After reading the cards in each pile, you may decide that some of the major points need beefing up or more details. If so, go back to your bibliography and dig up some more material. Adding material must be done at this point or not at all. Fortunately, by having started early, you now have time to do this additional research.

NUMBERING

Once you've decided that all systems are "go," you may then number all of your note slips from one to the end. Now you can begin writing.

WRITING YOUR PAPER

WRITING

With the cards in front of you and in order, begin writing rapidly and spontaneously as you can. Don't bog down by stopping to ponder alternatives. Just keep going!

INTRODUCTION

You need one, but don't spend time on it just yet. For now, a sentence or two is enough. Go on to writing the main body of the paper.

FOOTNOTES/ENDNOTES

They can come later, too. But, in the meantime, whenever you use information from a reference card, write the number of your reference card after the sentence in parentheses.

SUPPORTING MATERIAL

So, continue to write out the main points, but be sure to back them up. Each time you write a major point, you should strive to do the following.
1. State your point clearly at the outset.
2. Develop the point beyond a brief statement.

3. Support with quotes from authorities, statistics.
4. Illustrate with examples.
5. Link the major point with other ones in your paper.

FIRST DRAFT

After finishing this fast rough draft, don't leave it as such. You may be able to read it now, but, in a few days, it could look like hieroglyphics. That's why it's important to make a clean copy while you still understand what all your notations mean.

COOLING-OFF PERIOD

Now, put aside your clean copy for a couple of days. When you come back to it, you'll be better able to read it critically and make changes where needed.

FINAL DETAILS

EDITING

When you come back to your paper, editing is the next step. Editing can mean rearranging sentences, replacing awkward words, checking to see that the paragraphs flow smoothly from one to the next, even rewriting the entire paper may be necessary.

You have to be concerned enough to make the changes that will help express your points as clearly and as interestingly as possible. Here are some technical details that should be taken care of.

TRANSITIONS. Don't make it obvious to the reader that your paper was written from one note followed by another. Try to make the shift from point to point smooth and easy to follow.

GRAMMAR AND SPELLING. Often underrated, these two elements of writing can make or break your paper. Errors in grammar and spelling may divert the reader's attention from the strength of your paper's content to the weakness of its style.

SPELLING

Look over your entire paper for misspelled words. Use the dictionary to make sure you're right. If you're using a word processing program on a computer, use the spell-check. After you've done all you can, have a good speller read your paper. Misspelled words are bound to create a bad impression.

PLAGIARISM

(Using another person's words without acknowledgment.) Avoiding plagiarism is very simple. If you use someone else's words or ideas, just give the writer credit. Everyone has a distinctive writing style and way of thinking. The instructor who is grading your paper is bound to notice any changes in either.

FOOTNOTES/ENDNOTES

The main purpose of a footnote or endnote is to give credit to any information that you have quoted or paraphrased.

FOOTNOTE/ENDNOTE LOCATION

One commonly used method is to make a complete list of your cited notes and put them at the end of your paper. You'll still want to put a superscript (a number) at the end of every quoted or paraphrased line or paragraph. Ask your instructor where s/he wants the footnotes/endnotes to be placed.

TITLE

The title can be different from the topic line you've chosen. It is often a better idea to wait until you have finished your paper before coming up with an appropriate title. But, whatever the title, it should reflect the contents of your paper.

INTRODUCTION

Use your general purpose statement as the foundation for your introduction. State your purpose and explain how you plan to carry it out. Whatever you write, make sure it has something to do with your title and your conclusion.

CONCLUSION

Make sure you include a conclusion. Otherwise, the reader is apt to be left dangling. Often, the conclusion will be used to summarize or restate the paper's purpose. In this way, it refers back to the introduction.

FINAL COPY

Make it reflect all the work that you have put into your paper. Weeks of research can be ruined in minutes by a sloppy final copy. If your paper looks sloppy and disorganized, the instructor may conclude that your overall work has been sloppy and disorganized too.

Below are seven guidelines to improve the appearance of your final copy.

1. Use only one side of white paper.
2. Type your paper or use a word-processor or computer. Double space.
3. Leave ample margins for the instructor's comments.
4. If using a typewriter, erase your mistakes thoroughly or use correction tape. Don't strikeover.
5. Single space long quotations (five or more lines) indenting five spaces on each side. (Use no quotation marks with this format.)
6. Proofread carefully. Look for spelling errors, typos, and other flaws. If you use a spell-check on a computer, still check for unrecognized words, names, places, etc.
7. Hand in your paper on time. A late paper will lower your grade.

VOCABULARY: BUILDING A BACKGROUND

Definition: can-di-date—A person who seeks or is nominated for an office, prize, or honor.

> WORD HISTORY: *candidate*—originally, one clothed in white. In Latin *candidus* meant "glittering," "white." In ancient Rome, a man campaigning for office wore a white toga and was consequently called *candidatus*, "clothed in white." From this comes our word *candidate* with the meaning "one campaigning for office," but without the original significance as to dress.

WORDS IN CONTEXT

Directions: Make a light check mark (✓) alongside one of the two words (choices) that most nearly expresses the meaning of the italicized word in the episodes. (Answers are given on p. 126.) Excerpts reprinted courtesy of *SPORTS ILLUSTRATED*. Copyright ©, Time Inc. All rights reserved.

The NBA doesn't *sanction* trash talking, of course. Two years ago the league *instituted* a rule against *taunting*: Anyone caught shouting "in your face" or similar *epithet* could be hit with a technical foul and a $500 fine. The rule has had an effect. "Five hundred dollars for a technical, that's expensive, even for a millionaire," says Kendall Gill, the Nets' swingman.

96. doesn't *sanction*	approve	forbid
97. *instituted* a rule	abolished	established
98. against *taunting*	pushing	teasing
99. similar *epithet*	compliments	insults

Like Dominique Wilkins, Jumaine Jones, power forward of the Georgia Bulldogs, is a bit of a showman. He likes to *electrify* the crowds with an *assortment* of *thunderous* dunks, *resounding* *rejections* and three-point bombs. "The students love him," says Georgia coach, Ron Jirsa.

100. *electrify* the crowds	scare	thrill
101. *assortment* of dunks	routine	variety
102. *thunderous* dunks	fast	loud
103. *resounding* rejections	exciting	decisive
104. resounding *rejections*	blocks	fouls

Although the once *soporific* Cleveland Cavaliers have not exactly turned into the Harlem Globetrotters, they nevertheless averaged 98.5 points during the 10-game winning streak, compared to their 87.5 point average last season (lowest in the league).

105. once *soporific* Cavaliers	drowsy	lively

VOCABULARY ANSWERS

1. wild
2. admit
3. rash
4. offense
5. stands
6. rule
7. entails
8. struck lightly
9. disgrace
10. large
11. form
12. trinket
13. disappointed
14. revived
15. absolute
16. scant
17. restrained
18. inflammatory
19. person before
20. measure sound
21. trainee
22. small office
23. drives
24. performance
25. successive
26. discouraging
27. able
28. stimulator
29. dramatic
30. instructive
31. controlling
32. remembered
33. filled
34. standard
35. lecture

36. roundabout
37. name
38. inclination
39. showiness
40. preference
41. burned
42. attacking
43. insults
44. sinister
45. feeling
46. unbeatable
47. disappeared
48. melted
49. hopeless
50. filled
51. somber
52. thrashed
53. stingy
54. awesome
55. ribbed
56. quiet
57. overwhelming
58. vision
59. assorted
60. outstanding
61. first appearance
62. proof
63. self-possession
64. hopefulness
65. remarkably
66. plans
67. sticks to it
68. natural sense
69. varied
70. rebels

71. rejected
72. laughed at
73. includes
74. renovating
75. establishing
76. quick
77. detestable
78. feature
79. program
80. danger
81. beginning
82. uneasiness
83. teaching
84. extend
85. steered
86. enormous
87. pattern
88. emphasized
89. copy
90. jerky
91. loyalty
92. pardon
93. falling apart
94. spirit
95. bottomless
96. approve
97. established
98. teasing
99. insults
100. thrill
101. variety
102. loud
103. exciting
104. blocks
105. drowsy